YACHTING
MONTHLY

THE SAILOR'S
SIN BIN

YACHTING
MONTHLY

THE SAILOR'S SIN BIN

*Cruisers confess to their
boating blunders*

**ADLARD
COLES**

LONDON · OXFORD · NEW YORK · NEW DELHI · SYDNEY

ADLARD COLES
Bloomsbury Publishing Plc
50 Bedford Square, London, WC1B 3DP, UK
29 Earlsfort Terrace, Dublin 2, Ireland

BLOOMSBURY, ADLARD COLES and the Adlard Coles logo are trademarks
of Bloomsbury Publishing Plc

First published in Great Britain 2022

A catalogue record for this book is available from the British Library

Library of Congress Cataloguing-in-Publication data has been applied for

ISBN: PB: 978-1-3994-0287-3; ePub: 978-1-3994-0286-6; ePDF: 978-1-3994-0285-9

2 4 6 8 10 9 7 5 3 1

Design by Phillip Beresford

Typeset in Adobe Caslon Pro by Deanta Global Publishing Services, Chennai, India
Printed and bound in Great Britain by CPI Group (UK) Ltd., Croydon CR0 4YY

To find out more about our authors and books visit www.bloomsbury.com
and sign up for our newsletters

EDITOR'S INTRODUCTION

Worse things happen at sea, so the saying goes. As sailors, we all like to think of ourselves as experienced, knowledgeable, and above making silly mistakes. Of course, in reality, all of us make mistakes. We just hope that the consequences are not serious, and that no one was there to witness our embarrassment.

Even in a world of smartphone navigation and social media, shipwrecks and collisions, getting stuck in the toilet and cases of mistaken identity, worse things do indeed happen at sea. Mostly, they remain hidden until the skippers can bear the guilt no longer and must unburden their souls.

The *Yachting Monthly* Confessional has, for the last half-century, been hearing cruisers' confessions, offering absolution and sharing the blunders and shenanigans of real sailors for all to enjoy.

Everything you are about to read really did happen. While plenty of boats were damaged in the process, all of the sailors survived to tell the tale, allowing us to learn from their mistakes, while having a good laugh at their expense.

If this book brings your own nautical misdemeanours to mind, *Yachting Monthly* stands ready to hear your confession too!

Theo Stocker
Editor
Yachting Monthly

CONTENTS

1 POMP, CIRCUMSTANCE AND LOVE: Inflated egos get popped quickly at sea   **13**

Just a little more air • Roger Cooke   14

Peace shattered • Richard Morris   15

Shoe disposal service • Craig Robinson   15

A French delicacy • Patrick Hurd   16

Fender thieves • Brian Hewitt   17

Wedding thriller • Robert Cave   17

Sealed with a kiss • Colin Duce   18

Dinghy disaster • Simon Walsh   19

Circle of shame • Tom Mullarkey   20

Close encounter • Christopher Beaumont-Hutchings   20

Do you need a wally? • Alex Maioru   21

Better to keep quiet • Hamish Wills   22

You've been framed • Ian Burton   23

Caught out on camera • Roy Sheriff   24

Let me demonstrate! • David Sannella   24

Knot tested • Sir Robin Knox-Johnston   25

Local sights • Dermot Cox   26

Teaching aid • Paul Fearn   26

2   ROOKIE ERRORS: The beginners' mistakes we wish
    we didn't have to make   28

Asleep with the fishes • Ed Beard   29

Wind in your sails • Liz Carter   30

Jumping for joy • Angela Chapman   30

Dazzling sunglasses • Bill Gray   31

So long, silverware • Simon Ransome-Williams   31

Water ingress • FM Aalbersberg   32

Racing pedigree • Rob Nicholls   33

Boating lingo • Malcolm Kent   33

You say throw, I throw • Paul Russell   34

Magic carpets • Alan Douglas   35

Diesel dilemma • Harold Flannery   36

Feeling a jerk • Bill Gray   36

3   NAVIGATION NONSENSE: Finding your way is far
    from plain sailing   37

Sprightly septuagenarian • Anton Pruden   38

Pass the biscuits • Ella Walsworth-Bell   39

A foggy memory • Peter Adeline   40

Fire, fire! • Piers Pisani   40

A Fyne cock-up • Stewart May   41

Unlucky strike • David Beattie   42

Honk like you mean it • Terrence Kearney   42

Doing the time warp • Martin Lampard   43

Aerobatic signal • Alan Wilson   44

Not a tanker • Tommi Jokiniemi   45

Overly helpful sailor • Simon Vage   45

Into the blue • Kay 'Jay J' Bommer   46

**4 TO MOTOR OR NOT TO MOTOR: We didn't
need the engine anyway!**   **47**

International incident • Edward Sutton   48

Seagull serenade • Chris West   49

A well-mown carpet • Richard Clutterbuck   49

What a cock-up! • John Soloman   50

Just don't stop • Chris Hanson   51

Temperamental outboard • Glenn Johnstone   51

Cherbourg reverse • Brian Clements   53

Who needs a propeller? • Don Fitzroy-Smith   53

A wheelie bin disaster • David Hilton   54

Singing prop • Julian Brown   55

Oil mishap • Colin Flood   55

5 HIGH AND DRY: When the boat just won't float   **57**

Hull-deep in mud • Robin Hunter   58

Ready, steady, stop! • Susie Mellers   59

A silver lining • Gordon Fyfe   59

Road block • James Deasley   60

Ahh, it'll be fine! • Don Fitzroy Smith   61

Breakfast with a bump • George DuBose   62

Fruits de mer • Keith May   62

Watch your units • Andreas Fallaschinski   64

6 FAMILY FIASCOS: Dramas with our nearest and dearest   **65**

Tin cans needed • Ed Crosse   66

Doing a runner • David Pick   67

Service with a woof! • Beryl Chalmers   67

Push me pull you • Phillip Cave   68

Bottoms up • Brian North   69

Mum's the word • Timothy Long   70

A lesson in siphoning • Thomas Robinson   71

Strangers in the night • Ray Lupton   72

Don't forget your crew • Matthew Diggle   72

A little voice • Sylvie Dubois-Marshall   73

A humble apology • Colin Langford   74

7 A CLOSE SHAVE: How did they get away with it?   **75**

Going up in the world • James Frost   76

A shared teaspoon • Simon Temple   77

Mast mishap • Harry Blathwayt   77

A wheel of a time • Simon James   78

MOB finale • Rob Whelan   79

Locker legs • Paul Clarke   80

Dress for the occasion • Michael Davy   81

A sinking feeling • Liz Saunders   81

Holding on • Eilef J Gard   83

Almost a muddy end • Richard Hope-Hawkins   84

A skipper's prerogative • Terry Kemmann-Lane   85

Use your head • Martin Doxey   86

Whale spotting • Alistair Yeaman   86

8 DINGHY DISASTERS: Big cock-ups in small boats   **88**

Nothing to see here • Bill Brimble   89

Learning the hard way • Simon Lund   90

Flyaway dinghy • Susie Potter   90

Knot withstanding • Mike Howard   91

Romance in the rain • Peter Solly   92

The submersible dinghy • Nick Johnstone   93

Tender loving care • Lesley Black   94

Still waters • Andrew Robinson   96

Without a paddle • Tim Bultitude   96

Too slippery by half • Jack Handley   97

Lobster pot tango • Oliver L Shaw   98

Captain Underpants • Mark Cherrill   99

9 MOORING MAYHEM: Getting tied up in knots   **100**

Off the wall • Leonie Steer   101

Ignore at your peril • Therese Labos   102

High and dry • Huw Gibby   103

Don't pull that plug! • William H. Holliday   104

Newton's third law of motion • Christopher Hill   104

Prop walk lessons • Rob Ward   105

Something to ponder • Mike Thornton   106

Sink or swim • Ron Stoddart   106

Tied up in knots • Kevin West   108

Ice-cream distraction • Kelly Rashleigh   108

Dragging to windward • Keith Greenfield   109

A sideways two-step • Don Fitzroy Smith   110

10 THE COVER OF DARKNESS: Embarrassing episodes the night can't hide — **111**

Blinded by the light • Peter Rolt — 112

How'd that happen? • Graham Hughes — 113

Brightlingsea lights • Sarah O'Reilly — 113

What is that? • Liza Dodds — 114

Moonshine • Christopher Smith — 115

On the gas • George DuBose — 115

Rude awakening • Philip Cave — 116

Fog off Roscoff • Peter Kersey — 117

The big sleep • Richard Pearce — 117

11 TOILET HUMOUR: We shouldn't laugh, but... — **119**

Nappy hooligan • Terrence Kearney — 120

A drop in the bucket • Kurt Jewson — 121

The critical moment • Chris Mardon — 121

Bonnet de Douche • Richard Avent — 122

Soaked through • John Tylor — 123

The porcelain shrine • Paul Hough — 124

A messy business • Oliver L Shaw — 124

Morse code rescue • Geoff Evans — 125

Neighbourly swap • Peter Guinan — 126

Black tea, please • Peter Reid — 127

Morse code release • Oscar O'Sullivan — 127

1
POMP, CIRCUMSTANCE AND LOVE: INFLATED EGOS GET POPPED QUICKLY AT SEA

— JUST A LITTLE MORE AIR —

ROGER COOKE

His background was clearly military; his bearing suggested the parade ground and in speech, his certainty of tone conveyed the confidence of command. I had been invited to crew on his small cruiser moored on the River Hamble. To reach it we would use his tender which, he assured me, was ready waiting alongside the pontoon. It was one of those curious yellow inflatable objects that seems unable to decide whether it's a child's toy or something with greater pretensions. It lay limply in the water.

'Surely you don't mean us to use that?' I asked.

'Nothing wrong with it,' he replied. 'Perfectly adequate when handled in a seaman-like manner.'

'At the very least, it needs to be fully inflated,' I advised.

'It's a mistake to over-inflate them. They firm up when you get in.'

'After you...' I said.

With a look of steely confidence and a hint of disdain for my timidity, he stepped into the dinghy's centre. The ends rose up and clasped him lovingly round the thighs.

'I think,' he said thoughtfully, 'perhaps just a little more air.'

For a few glorious seconds, the ensemble maintained its unlikely state of equilibrium... and then collapsed into the Hamble. I also collapsed.

— PEACE SHATTERED —

RICHARD MORRIS

Sailing from Alicante to Menorca, I anchored in a quiet bay off Tagomago Island at the north of Ibiza. I opened my book and enjoyed the peace and quiet. Whereupon a horde of small motorboats arrived, loudly playing music, drinking and boisterously having fun. My peace shattered, I was irritated. So I decided to swim in the beautiful warm water.

That was fine, until I started being attacked – very painfully – by jellyfish. I was far from my boat and, being near to the motorboats, I climbed up a stern ladder to the surprise of those on board.

'Medusa, medusa,' I explained in my best Spanish.

They said I could stay to compose myself after my panic, gave me a beer, and in truth the music took my mind off things. Half an hour later, a dinghy from another motorboat kindly rowed me back to my boat.

Somewhat sheepishly, I said 'Gracias' and climbed on board.

— SHOE DISPOSAL SERVICE —

CRAIG ROBINSON

My wife and I helped our friends to relaunch their boat. It was full of tools, drop cloths and bin bags. They were about to sail from Anglesey to Ireland for a wedding, on a three-week trip. I loaded their tools and bin bags into my car and wished them bon voyage.

We were excited for them because their project had taken a lot of time and money. They had all of their glad rags, wedding presents, provisions, charts, in fact everything they needed for a fabulous holiday.

They disappeared from view and I headed to the nearest municipal tip with a car load of rubbish. All was well, until the next day when they called and asked if I still had the bin bags – of course, I didn't.

The phone went silent. Shortly, they explained they had run out of packing space and put all of their shoes – wedding, everyday, boating and walking around, nearly their entire wardrobe of shoes – in a black bag for ease of handling. They had to go shoe shopping the next day.

— A FRENCH DELICACY —

PATRICK HURD

Many years ago now, when young and carefree, I was part of a crew with my two older brothers, sailing a Westerly GK 29 from Corsica to Cassis in the south of France. It had been a gentle sail, with nothing much to report and, being the youngest brother, of course I was given the 0200 till 0500 watch.

Because the seas were calm, at the end of my watch I went into the fore peak to sleep and as it was warm, took my clothes off, not expecting to arrive at our destination for a good few hours. I awoke to a glorious day, the forehatch was open, but I hadn't noticed that we had stopped moving. The GK's fore peak is quite low, so when standing on the bunks… need I say more.

I stood up only to be facing the quayside cafés, full with people, now choking on their coffee. While asleep, we had moored bows to the harbour wall (which you could do in those days). It's taken me this long to come to terms with what was a very embarrassing moment!

— FENDER THIEVES —

BRIAN HEWITT

A couple of years ago, nine of us sailor friends chartered a very nice Lagoon 480 from Gouvia Marina near Corfu. I hopped in the tender and eagerly circumnavigated the yacht with my trusty GoPro on record. We then took in the gorgeous sights of Paxos and Anti Paxos.

One day when we were berthed and had gone ashore for lunch, we saw another yacht raft up against us. After climbing back on board we realised my wife's brand new Musto slip shoes had been stolen. When we returned the yacht to the charter company, they told us we had lost one of the big blue fenders and threatened to retain the £3k deposit unless we paid up.

'There were two fenders when you left,' they argued profusely; we argued hard to the contrary.

As soon as I got home I popped the memory card out of the GoPro and into the TV. There they were: two big blue fenders – the charter guys had been right all along. The yacht which rafted against us, and stole the wife's shoes, must have taken the big blue fender too. Doh!

— WEDDING THRILLER —

ROBERT CAVE

This is one of my most embarrassing stories. It started with one of those very hot, almost entirely windless days. I had a 25-mile sail ahead of me and I was in no rush. I set the lightest and largest sail, a cruising chute, Big Orange, as

I call it, and goosewinged dead downwind. Big Orange has the disadvantage that it hides everything behind it, but in light airs it's brilliant.

There I was, making one knot through the water, autopilot on and listening to the mp3 player through my earphones. The boat doesn't have large water tanks, so while I am away I try to minimise laundry by wearing as little as possible. Well, that's my excuse.

On this occasion I was wearing nothing, which was fine as there was nothing around me for miles and miles. Just then, a Michael Jackson song started playing through my headphones and I couldn't help dancing. I was really going for it, prancing around in the middle of the cockpit, though Jackson's 360° spin takes me four jumps to get all the way around.

Just as I threw my head back and started singing out loud, a sight-seeing boat appeared from behind the big orange sail, and on the bow were a bride and groom, having photos taken with my boat as a backdrop, while the rest of the wedding party stared agog at the sight of me on deck.

I hope I didn't ruin too many of the photos, or that a video of the incident doesn't crop up online. I'll keep a better lookout next time.

— SEALED WITH A KISS —

COLIN DUCE

Following a rough crossing to Ostend with my girlfriend Julie, I was on borrowed time. We had left Ramsgate in my Mystere 26 in calm conditions but were forecast a Force 7 later. My sensible dad would follow the next day in his motorboat. We eventually surfed into Ostend, having taken far too long. Julie was in bits, and I was not in her good books. The next day, it was calm sailing from Ostend into delightful Holland. Maybe I could earn back some of my lost marks?

We were motoring along the very straight Kanaal door Walcheren. Dad had gone on ahead and would meet us at the lock. Julie was next to me in the cockpit and a rush of exuberance overtook me, and I thought I would try for a make-up snog. It worked! All was well until I looked up and realised the boat had turned 90 degrees and we ran hard aground just before hitting the bank.

I don't know which was worse, Julie's withering look or having to call Dad and ask him to come and tow us off. Julie eventually became my wife but caught the ferry home.

— DINGHY DISASTER —

SIMON WALSH

Sailing a dinghy in Menorca, I turned up at the office with my various certificates to show how qualified I was, but as it was really quite windy, I decided I would go out later in the day with an instructor. I'm happy enough in a stable 30ft yacht, but 12ft of wobbly dinghy for a large lad like me is another thing.

Anyway, out we went and even with the main reefed and the jib partly furled it flew! I was happily chatting with the instructor when the wind dropped suddenly. As the dinghy lurched towards me, I accidentally gybed, with me on the wrong side of the boat.

We were over at right angles in the blink of an eye – my extra ballast had worked wonders. The young woman looked at me, possibly in awe of my incompetence, but remained calm and with the boat upright again we carried on. Tacking back towards the shore, a crowd came out to watch us turning up to wind and stopping on the mooring buoy. The instructor jumped out to tie off, and, feeling energised, I stood up and cracked my head on the boom with a resounding hollow clang. The instructor looked up with concern, at which point I stepped back and fell head over heels over the transom. I may have imagined the spectators trying not to laugh, but it was a damp walk of shame back to the office.

— CIRCLE OF SHAME —

TOM MULLARKEY

We were moored on a buoy in Lamlash Bay off Arran. My habitual desire to get going had been thwarted by requests from my son and his friend for another bacon sarnie and leaving my wife and these two below, I demonstrated my impatience by prepping the boat for departure on my own.

Having started the engine, I went below to the heads, emerging a few minutes later to see masts going by and the crew looking out of their portlights in bemusement. I leapt on deck to take the boat out of gear and it slowed its circles, at three knots, around the buoy. Looking up, I then saw that the crew of every boat in the bay was on deck, while the shoreline was packed with people observing this phenomenal piece of seamanship.

— CLOSE ENCOUNTER —

CHRISTOPHER BEAUMONT-HUTCHINGS

This happened to me some years back. I understand that old Charlie Tango is still up to the same old tricks to this day! I had flown out to join my parents who, having just completed the Atlantic Rally for Cruisers (ARC), were cruising in company with their friends Chris and Jo.

After a spirited day's sailing to St Vincent we arrived at Young Island Cut and accepted two mooring buoys from a local entrepreneur, 'Charlie Tango', who assured us they had enough swinging room.

After a customarily raucous evening I awoke in the early hours to a noise and upon clambering out of my hatch discovered the stern of Chris and Jo's boat about to collide with us amidships. Having had the importance of pristine gel coat instilled from a young age I vaulted the guardrail down on to their stern platform without a second thought. Jo materialised out of the darkness and we averted the impending collision.

A gust of wind then suddenly carried the two boats well apart. Leaving me – in just my boxer shorts – stranded on the wrong boat alongside Jo – in

her nightwear – just as her husband appeared on deck enquiring: 'What the bloody hell is going on here?'

It's unclear to this day whether our account of the near-calamity was fully believed.

– DO YOU NEED A WALLY? –

ALEX MAIORU

I would like to share with fellow readers the darkest, most embarrassing moment of my sailing life. We were in Lefkas in Greece. A boat was coming in stern-to next to us, with a nice young couple from the Netherlands on board. By the time I put down the gin and tonic to help with the lines, the nimble lass was already on the quay, tying the windward mooring line. No drama, I said to myself, wondering about the curious way of holding the line with her foot while her partner was throwing the other mooring line.

They had it all under control, so more from friendly neighbourliness than any real need, I asked, 'Can I give you a hand?'

She looked puzzled, so I checked the ensign quickly. Yep, they were Dutch, so they must speak English.

'Do you need a hand?' I insisted.

Another blank look for an answer.

'Do you need h-e-l-p?'

She exchanged a few words with her partner in a language I couldn't understand, let alone recognise. So I took the second line and made it fast.

'Welcome to Lefkas,' I said, stepping on my plank, back aboard to continue enjoying my drink and thought nothing of it.

Come dinner time at a lovely tavern, our handsome Dutch neighbours strolled past and my wife and I waved. They returned the gesture and only at that point did I notice. The dark earth could not crack a hole deep enough for me to crawl into its melting flames. I realised that the Dutch girl had no hand on one arm and a just a couple of fingers on the other, which I presumed to be a birth defect.

More than 15 years later, I still feel terrible for the lousiest and most insensitive few minutes of my life. I'm a worm without a rock. I sincerely apologise to the charming young lady for my temporary lapse of vision. On the upside, I am now always look at a person's hands before I ask if they want help with the lines.

— BETTER TO KEEP QUIET —

HAMISH WILLS

My son was proudly telling his colleague and keen sailing friend from a wealthy family all about the big step that I, his dad, had taken getting into yachting. He explained that at 22ft, I had just bought a little boat to start with, with basic navigation instruments, pretty tight cabin space and a temperamental outboard. He went on about how the weather had smiled down upon us on our first trip to Dartmouth, how faultless our navigation had been, how enjoyable the evening beers were as the sun went down and how perfect our mooring had been at the end of the day.

His friend listened patiently and politely to the end before mentioning that his dad had just got into yachting too and bought himself a boat.

'What is it?' asked my son, with a great deal of interest.

'It's a 104ft motorsailer berthed in Greece with a permanent crew, two masts and two powered tenders.'

'I should have known that he'd have had a story like that and kept quiet!' said my son.

— YOU'VE BEEN FRAMED —

IAN BURTON

'Use the lock to reach your masthead,' said a friend in Portishead Marina control. Tide out, I heeled the boat over and replaced my faulty VHF antenna. Motoring astern, I manoeuvred my Eygthene 24 back into the marina in the warm sun with that confident glow you get with your first boat, one bare foot placed casually on the tiller ready to fend off the harbour wall, arms outstretched to turn back to my berth.

The night before was cool, and now everything had a covering of dew, including my deck. As I pushed off the wall, my feet slipped, dumping me like a stricken tortoise.

In the fall, I kicked my throttle lever fully forward. Trying to get up, I blindly grasped the tiller, flinging it hard over. I looked up to see my bow narrowly miss the solid wall opposite, with my friend watching on, trying not to laugh. My sunglasses sat twisted on my head as I gathered myself, looked around and asked my friend in the marina to delete the security footage.

'No,' he said, probably trying to remember his YouTube password. Only inches away from absolute disaster, I learned the best lesson ever: don't ever try to look cool – it will backfire.

– CAUGHT OUT ON CAMERA –

ROY SHERIFF

I decided to make a video showing how to enter and leave moorings in the Dee estuary. On a calm day, when the buoys were clearly visible and camera shake minimal, the leaving bit worked well. But on the way back, eyes fixed on the viewfinder, I left the helming to crew. Picking out the channel buoys using close-ups and panoramic views, my narration went something like:

'As you head down the buoyed channel, you'll see off your starboard bow a red fishing boat… Where's it gone?'

Taking my eyes from the viewfinder, the red fishing boat was some distance off our port bow and we were headed for the largest sandbank in the area on an ebbing tide. With less than a metre underneath, we dropped all sails, engine going as fast as we could to the marked channel, hoping we'd still have enough water to make it back to the mooring. Needless to say, the video was never used!

– LET ME DEMONSTRATE! –

DAVID SANNELLA

I was out with a novice friend in my *Yachting Monthly* Senior Trumpet Coyote on Lake Union in Seattle. I was being all expert and teaching her to sail. The winds were light and the sun bright. At the southern end of the lake, NOAA (the American Met Office) used to moor their large research ships.

We sailed nearby one and I was trying to show her how not to get too close and manoeuvre out of a possible problem. Well, a little rogue gust came out of nowhere and pushed me straight into the large ship. The top of my mast scraped along its bow as I tried to get out of there, anxious I would snag its anchoring gear. The noise it produced was prodigiously loud for such a small boat and I was afraid that a NOAA crew member would hear it. No one noticed, but I'm certain that eventually someone will see the scrape marks and wonder where they came from. So much for expert instruction!

— KNOT TESTED —

SIR ROBIN KNOX-JOHNSTON

One of my ways of checking people for the Clipper Round The World Race is to make sure they can tie knots. There are certain ones they have to know as part of their four-week training. I remember going down to a boat and asking a lady who had just joined to do a bowline.

She said, 'I haven't done one for nine months', and I was absolutely furious.

I said, 'Come on, you're about to cross the Pacific Ocean and you haven't been keeping up with your training, you're a danger to yourself and to your fellow crew members.'

And she started arguing with me, then she realised the other two ladies who were there were on my side.

So I said, 'Right, I'll be down tomorrow and you'll show me all six of those knots.'

Of course, I went down the next day and I couldn't remember which boat she was on, so she got away with it!

– LOCAL SIGHTS –

DERMOT COX

We had finally launched our boat after the first COVID lockdown when I received a call to attend hospital for surgery; another two months of the season lost! Finally, fit and ready to sail, my wife and I made our way out to our mooring, situated close to Portsmouth Harbour entrance, nearly abeam of the aircraft carriers.

After so long an absence we carefully checked over the boat. All was well, except for extensive weed fouling the propeller. No option for it, bathers on, over the side and a few cool minutes later our prop was clear.

My wife was below while I towelled off in solitary splendour, enjoying the sunny cockpit. Having hung up the towel I leant over to reach for my boxers, when from over the rail could be heard: 'And now, ladies and gentlemen, if you look to starboard you will see...'

Well, one can only hope all the sightseers aboard the harbour tour boat were looking to starboard! They don't usually pass that close to our trot; perhaps they won't be tempted to again.

– TEACHING AID –

PAUL FEARN

I have been delivering yachts and teaching beginners to sail for many years now, so I have a fairly deep well of embarrassing moments – it goes with the job. But it was an incident in the classroom that comes to mind most often.

About two years ago I found myself in the classroom, standing in front of about eight potential Day Skippers, eager to start the first day of their theory course. Unusually, the class was comprised mainly of middle-aged women, two teenage daughters and a token man. I was running through the equipment that we would be using and pointed out that they had all equipped themselves with the standard Portland course plotter, while I had the smaller but more flexible RYA Handy Plotter. As I was waving my plotter around, the words that came out of my mouth were, 'And I've got a small floppy one.'

The silence that followed lasted about one second, followed by uproar and raucous laughter. A great ice-breaker, the rest of the course was a joy to teach.

2
ROOKIE ERRORS: THE BEGINNERS' MISTAKES WE WISH WE DIDN'T HAVE TO MAKE

———

— ASLEEP WITH THE FISHES —

ED BEARD

The veteran skipper of a successful racing yacht invited me to join his seasoned crew for an offshore season. As a novice to high performance sailing, I was eager to show everyone how helpful and competent I could really be.

Before long I was promoted from winch-grinding to galley mate. Although my porridge was reviewed as having 'plaster of Paris consistency', my early efforts paid off as I began to earn the crew's trust and respect.

This changed during one particularly hard-fought race from England to France, when the bowman called through the howling wind and driving rain: 'Bring up the bag for the jib!'

With customary enthusiasm I dove below deck to search for it. No luck. In the darkness, the heavy-duty blue sail bag had all but vanished, hidden amid piles of spare sails. As the swell of the sea tossed me around the pitching cabin, I grew impatient and frustrated at my failure in this critical moment. Just then, my flailing hands grazed rough canvas, and I could just make out that it was blue – success!

I grasped it and heaved it up onto the deck, before holding it triumphantly aloft in the cockpit before the assembled crew. It was not the sail bag. It was the blue sack used to stow the crew's sleeping bags. At that moment, a powerful gust of breeze forced the bag wide open and a dozen sleeping bags billowed out into the English Channel. I am still waiting for my invite back.

— WIND IN YOUR SAILS —

LIZ CARTER

In 1974, my husband and I started sailing on the lakes in Berlin on our lovely Silhouette. A friend helped us rig her and took us out for our first sailing lesson, jumping ship at a convenient jetty, leaving two novices learning to sail by trial and error. The method we used to get back on our mooring was with our trusty Seagull outboard.

The next Sunday, we went out for another sail and were definitely getting the hang of it until it was time to return to our mooring.

In those distant times, motors were banned on River Havel on alternate weekends so we had to sail back. Naturally, we had to sail upwind. Tacking as close as possible, we let the sails go, put the bow into the mooring and before we could grab anything, whoosh! We were going backwards at a rate of knots.

The commodore and committee, watching the racing from the clubhouse, looked pained. Sailors on the shore were shouting advice. At least, I think it was advice.

Eventually, sails trimmed, we were ready for attempt two. We didn't go for a drink in the clubhouse that night.

— JUMPING FOR JOY —

ANGELA CHAPMAN

We were bringing home our first sailing cruiser from the Hamble to our berth in Chichester. The day we chose wasn't ideal – the tide and wind were against us, and the crew (me) was inexperienced and nervous.

After several hours' motoring, we scraped across the Chichester harbour bar just before the lowest tide of the year. It was nearly dark. I was exhausted and couldn't wait to reach dry land.

At last we crept into our berth. Yay, we were home! I grabbed the mooring line, ready to leap ashore, when I realised I didn't know how to get off the boat – I was used to something much smaller. I panicked and leapt over the pulpit – no mean feat when you are 5ft 2in.

As I tumbled towards the pontoon, my foot unplugged next door's boat's electricity supply and I landed in a heap on the pontoon. Fortunately they weren't on board. I thought I had got away with it when I saw movement from the motor cruiser opposite. Their curtains were twitching, and they had clearly seen the whole escapade.

I grabbed my things, and my husband, and made a hasty escape!

— DAZZLING SUNGLASSES —

BILL GRAY

Day one of our annual sailing holiday in Greece and the early morning wind had died, so we furled the genoa and motored for a lunchtime stop in a small but busy anchorage. As we entered the bay, we seemed to attract some interest. I was slightly confused by this but assumed it was our crews' matching yellow sunglasses...

We briefly recced the bay and dropped the hook. I was surprised at how much the yacht seemed to be moving around the anchor. I left the cockpit to go forward to check the anchor chain and, as I ducked out from under the bimini, I realised the mainsail was still up! No wonder our arrival in the bay was interesting – and no surprise we were sailing around the anchor! When we left the anchorage after lunch, we did so under sail – I tried to pretend that when we arrived earlier we had also anchored under sail, but I don't think anyone was fooled.

— SO LONG, SILVERWARE —

SIMON RANSOME-WILLIAMS

In the summer of 1988, I flew out to Rhode Island, USA to help sail the 30ft racing trimaran *Caledonia* back to the UK. *Caledonia* was very sensitive to weight, so stores were kept to a minimum.

This was my first-ever ocean crossing and I was extremely nervous as we set out. On about my third watch, alone on deck, I was just finishing the washing up in the bucket designated for that purpose and reflecting on how well I thought I was coping. I looked at the gleaming plates and singular cooking pot in front of me and, swilling the bucket, I tossed the remaining dirty water over the stern. Immediately I realised my mistake and I watched in horror as the one knife, fork and spoon per person leapt, salmon-like, from the bucket into the Atlantic.

The icy reception I got from my crew mates each time we ate using only the cooking utensils as cutlery lasted until we got to the Azores. The ribbing has lasted a lifetime. I have learnt to incorporate the old carpenter's adage of 'measure twice, cut once' into all my sailing since.

— WATER INGRESS —

FM AALBERSBERG

When I was 13, I sailed an 8ft dinghy on a shallow inland lake. Having got stuck before, I decided to leave the retractable centreboard ashore as I did not see the benefit of a piece of wood sticking out under the boat anyway.

With hindsight, that must have had quite a negative effect on drift, but what bothered me more was the water coming in through the now empty slot.

Water sloshed in at every wave. As the boat slowly filled up, it became clear I would not make it back afloat, so I entered a nearby marina chandlery, dripping from the waist down. I said there was a hole in my boat and I needed to fix it.

The salesman, shocked at my appearance, my age, and my apparent intention to continue sailing with a leak, refused to sell me anything. Instead, he lectured me on seaworthiness and told me to get the boat out of the water and professionally repaired.

So I left, angry, and entered the nearest hardware store I could find: 'I'd like a bucket and a roll of duct tape, don't ask why!'

I taped the slot, emptied the dinghy and made it home before dinner.

— RACING PEDIGREE —

ROB NICHOLLS

My wife and I had just completed our Day Skipper and Competent Crew courses, and having bought a lovely Westerly Centaur a few months earlier, invited the other candidates for a day sail around the Solent.

In preparation for our first full sailing season I had updated the Centaur with its own chart plotter and digital speed/depth/log. Not one for reading instructions, I happily bashed away at the touchscreen until a map and some numbers appeared.

On a spring tide ebb and 2,000 rpm on the Beta 20, the little Centaur screamed out of Portsmouth Harbour with four fresh-faced Day Skippers aboard, at an impressive eight knots – despite the ancient and baggy sails.

I declared that we must have lucked in and that she was of racing pedigree. For the rest of the season, I regularly remarked to others that our average cruising speed wasn't far off planing. Months later I read the chart plotter instructions and realised that the Speed Through Water had been set to kilometres per hour. We had been bobbing along at four knots.

— BOATING LINGO —

MALCOLM KENT

The importance of communication cannot be overstated. It really is crucial to be clear in one's instructions, especially when communicating with someone who may not know the boating lingo.

On a trip through the Caledonian Canal we were in the same lock as a yacht crewed by an experienced skipper and his obviously not-so-experienced friend.

Due to COVID-19 restrictions the canal staff were not providing their usual level of service in handling lines, meaning that there was more risk than normal in negotiating the swirling waters of the locks, especially with just two on board.

The inexperienced crewman on the bow was not aware of the risk of leaving the lines a bit too slack, leaving the boat at the mercy of the sluices, so at one point the boat was heading for a crunch on the lock wall.

'Fend us off!' cried the skipper while wrestling with the stern line, wheel and gear lever. Imagine the sinking feeling he must have experienced when he next looked up, only to see the foredeck crew busily taking the fenders off.

— YOU SAY THROW, I THROW —

PAUL RUSSELL

After an arduous ten-hour completion of a recent Round the Island Race, *White Mistral* and its crew were making passage back to our Haslar mooring, and more

importantly, the pub. We noticed a small 24ft sailing yacht in dire straits off Gilkicker Point. It had been dismasted and its engine had also ceased working. At the helm was a young woman, seemingly all alone. Feeling chivalrous and intrigued, we felt compelled to render assistance.

It was clear that the powerless vessel would soon be in peril, so in a flash *White Mistral*'s skipper and owner dived into the starboard locker and threw me a long coiled rope. He grabbed the helm and shouted instructions that as we passed, I was to throw the line to the stricken vessel. As we motored and positioned ourselves alongside the vessel, cautious to avoid any of the rigging debris in the water, on the command 'Throw!', I duly and diligently took aim and launched the rope to the troubled yacht.

My efforts were met with incredulous looks on both *White Mistral*'s and the stricken yacht's skipper's face – who had now returned to the helm after working on his failed engine – as we passed each other, and simply kept going! I had not attached the end of the line to our boat, scuppering the towing process. Fluent Anglo-Saxon was uttered by my skipper as we had to undertake another risky pass to collect the tow rope. Thanks to his skill, the stricken yacht accepted our tow on the second attempt. We took it into Haslar and the grateful crew got the first round in that evening to thank us for our troubles.

We still discuss this incident frequently. The skipper believes that common sense required me to attach at least one end of the rope before throwing, though I maintain I simply did exactly what an experienced skipper told me to do.

— MAGIC CARPETS —

ALAN DOUGLAS

My first boat was a fine old Colvic cruiser called *Gefion*. I'd arranged for friends to come out on the river for the day and thought it a great idea to fill up the water tank. So I put in the hose and let it run, waiting for the water to pour out of the overflow pipe. Just before out guests arrived, my ten-year-old daughter asked me matter-of-factly, 'Daddy, why are the carpets floating?'

It turned out the water filler cap was only loosely attached and had no seal on it!

— DIESEL DILEMMA —

HAROLD FLANNERY

We were refuelling in Marseille and the attendant was in a rush. I have two tanks, and took the hose and put diesel in the starboard tank. Unbeknown to me, the attendant gave another hose to my friend, who filled up the port tank. When I checked the levels I found the port tank had not been filled. To my horror the diesel had gone into the water tank.

We pumped out into containers and wheeled them to the disposal tank and added lots of detergent. I asked my friend how it happened. He said he put diesel in the white cap as the red cap is for red diesel, which you cannot get in France! My wife now refuses to drink from the water tank.

— FEELING A JERK —

BILL GRAY

On a long passage across Lyme Bay with some mates a few summers ago, we decided to break out the fishing gear to see if we could catch some mackerel. One of my crew, Chris, wanted to try trolling for fish for the first time. With the handline deployed, he held on to the line expectantly. Chris was unsure how he would know when there was a fish on the line, so I told him that he would 'feel a jerk' and that he should then pull in the line immediately.

Chris soon got bored and although he was still holding the line, his attention was elsewhere. In full view of all the crew except Chris, I leaned over the stern and gave the fishing line a sharp tug. Full of excitement, Chris duly recovered the line, only to reveal no fish, of course. For the next hour, I repeated this five or six times before Chris got bored and packed away the fishing kit.

I'm still not sure if he knows…

3
NAVIGATION NONSENSE: FINDING YOUR WAY IS FAR FROM PLAIN SAILING

———

-SPRIGHTLY SEPTUAGENARIAN-

ANTON PRUDEN

The long-planned Baltic cruise had been finally realised. We and our family's dear old Macwester Wight 30ft ketch *Raniki* had enjoyed the crystal-clear waters. But now it was time to return.

My son, his friend and I took over from my father midway down the Kiel Canal. We entered Brunsbüttel lock and the Elbe estuary, bound for Cuxhaven. The old laptop we used as primary navigation was a bit dodgy so I had dug out some old charts. As the busy shipping lane approached, I turned to go astern of a merchantman, just cutting off the buoyed channel. The chart showed plenty of water. At five knots, it is surprising how quickly a heavy yacht can stop when its bilge keel buries itself in mud.

The stationary boat spun and lurched as we dropped the sails and started the engine. Another freighter passed alarmingly close. I feared for our safety and called up on the radio. A coastguard RIB approached but immediately went aground. We dried out rapidly, settling into the mud for the night.

It was just after dawn when we arrived at the Cuxhaven marina visitor berths; about the same time as the police, who wished to see my skipper's ticket. My paperwork was at home but I produced my father's. They looked a bit surprised – I was supposedly in my late 70s but was actually 50 at the time – but also relieved. Their job was done, I guess!

– PASS THE BISCUITS –

ELLA WALSWORTH-BELL

We'd crammed an extra family aboard for a day trip. Five children and three adults on our Moody 336. I'd promised my friend Lucy this sail all season, now it was mid-September.

'We don't have to go far, do we?' my husband asked quietly as the engine started.

'No.' I glanced across the flat water to the village opposite the moorings. We'd be there in a flash; anchor off and let the kids jump in the sea, while we'd have a cuppa. We weaved our way out through the moorings. Small excited faces sprouted in the companionway, 'Where're we going?' 'Can I steer?'

I picked the calmest of the bunch. 'Clara – you can go first.'

She bravely clutched the wheel. The others stood up for a better view, obscuring the instrument panel.

'Got the tide table?' I called to hubby, who was putting the kettle on.

'On the chart table.'

'Erm, no, it's not.'

I sighed and nipped down to grab it. Hmmm. Just before low water. Springs, as well.

'Lucy,' I shouted up, 'could you check the depth for me? Third instrument along. It should say one point something.'

'Ah. Nought point five... nought point three.'

My heart sank. Clara gripped the wheel with her tiny hands. Crunch – we grounded.

'Oops,' I said quietly.

'How long?' my husband asked.

'Erm. Best pass out that tea.'

'Anyone fancy a biscuit?' Lucy rustled her handbag.

'I've got plenty. This is so peaceful, sailing. Almost like we're not moving at all.'

— A FOGGY MEMORY —

PETER ADELINE

After a few years landbound, I'd bought a cracking little Sadler, and was desperately keen to put its shoulder to the wind. It was gloriously sunny at home in Emsworth, the forecast was perfect, and in no time at all we were off West Pole Beacon, sheets straining, sails pulling, bustling over to Bembridge.

I noted that the Isle of Wight was no longer visible. Hmm. Glancing over my shoulder, I was horrified to see thick banks of fog piling in from the south. In moments I was engulfed. I knew my options but didn't fancy any of them. The screen of the tiny heritage chart plotter was totally obscured by condensation.

I am old school, paper not pixels, and at that point had never even used a chart plotter. Then I remembered my phone and the Navionics app I'd bought out of curiosity. No better time to get on to the learning curve. Phone in one hand, tiller in the other, we crept back into Chichester Harbour, where it was gloriously sunny despite the menacing fog to the south.

The lesson? I'd only checked the land forecast. No mention of fog. Unlike the shipping forecast.

— FIRE, FIRE! —

PIERS PISANI

One weekend, my wife and I were gliding past the Sunseekers at Poole Quay in our new-to-us yacht when the engine alarm went off. Unable to leave the helm, I reduced revs and asked my wife to go below and let me know what the panel said.

She yelled back, 'FIRE, it says FIRE!'

'What?' I said. 'But it can't!'

But my wife, now adamant, yelled louder, 'It says FIRE, FIRE!'

I charged down the hatch, trying to recall how to use the extinguisher. I looked across and saw 'FIRE' was in fact 'FIRE FM', the local radio station displayed in graphics on the radio. The panel indicated a mere overheat!

— A FYNE COCK-UP —

STEWART MAY

The shingle beach south of Strachur, Loch Fyne, was our chosen spot for the early season launch of *Fyner Times*, a beautiful Pandora International.

A local jack-of-all-trades with a tractor kindly reversed the trailer down to the water's edge at low water, the plan being that we would return a few hours later with the tender, climb aboard and wait for high water to lift the boat off.

We returned to our humble abode, drank tea and ate biscuits as we chatted about how the wind was picking up and how good the sail to the mooring would be. It was soon time to head back and by our reckoning we were two hours before high water; plenty of time.

Driving along the coastal road gazing into the loch my blood suddenly ran cold.

'Who attached the boat to the trailer?' I asked. Three sets of eyes peered from the van as *Fyner Times*, resplendent in Mauritius blue, made its own way down the loch. I would describe what ensued as 'slapstick', but we caught up with the boat, and no damage was done. More importantly, no one saw and nobody knows!

— UNLUCKY STRIKE —

DAVID BEATTIE

It was 1983, I was in Jakarta, and my girlfriend had come to visit. I borrowed *Moonfleet*, a 23ft yacht with a petrol engine. We set off for one of the Pulau Seribu islands to moor for the night, without a chart or radio. Going out we nearly hit a reef, and the pilotage into the mooring against strong sunlight was difficult. That night a tropical storm hit. We fled ashore to shelter and watched lightning strike *Moonfleet*, illuminating the rigging.

Next morning, engineless, we sailed out through the reefs and headed back towards Tanjung Priok, Jakarta's port. The wind dropped and we stopped. At dusk the wind returned and we beat back towards the harbour, sailing between bamboo fishing platforms and anchored liners once used for the hajj. It was thrilling stuff as the wind increased and, with no lights showing, things appeared on our bow very quickly. We sailed through the entrance on a reach and finally beached in a muddy creek, as it was too narrow to sail. I say 'creek', but really it was an open sewer.

Here we sat, wondering what to do, until eventually the yard boys found us and spent an hour failing to start the engine.

It didn't put us off — we now sail a Westerly Konsort in the Solent.

— HONK LIKE YOU MEAN IT —

TERRENCE KEARNEY

Years ago, while visiting New York, I came across a shop that sold quirky gimmicks for cars. 'Make your car horn sound like an ocean liner' was the ad, so I bought it.

Years later my wife and family were leaving Poole Harbour in our Verl 900. The forecast was for light winds and potential fog, and we were heading for Cowes via the Needles. Halfway across Poole Bay heavy fog descended and visibility was down to ten metres. Out came the New York car horn, now converted to an electric foghorn. My son was designated to operate one six-second blast every 120 seconds.

As we approached the Needles the fog instantly cleared, and we could see about six yachts all with a lookout frantically scouring the horizon with binoculars for the *QE2*. The horn was quickly put away and I too scoured astern with binoculars, pretending it wasn't me. Apparently hidden in the regs there is a rule regarding the tone of foghorns and the size of vessel.

– DOING THE TIME WARP –

MARTIN LAMPARD

A long time ago, as a student, I received a phone call inviting me to crew on the Cowes–Dinard race. They had just fitted an early pre-GPS satellite navigation system, and as youngest crewman, and an electronics student to boot, I was assigned to be 'satnav operator'. We completed the race across successfully without incident or distinction. We encountered the usual hazy visibility around the Channel Islands and St Malo, but the satnav, with its fixes whose accuracy depended on the availability of visible satellites, backed up our increasingly lax estimated positions. I proudly and confidently informed the rest of the crew of our exact latitude and longitude, precise to three decimal places with error ranges that were frequently less than half a mile! They were all suitably impressed.

In advance of our departure on the morning of my birthday, I carefully initialised the satnav according to the instructions to give it time to start locking on to satellites. Visibility was forecast to be moderate at best, so I didn't want to take any chances.

We passed Jersey without incident, then things started to thicken up a bit and we lost sight of land. I started plotting the satnav positions on the chart and when the cockpit sang out, 'I think I can see land roughly due north', I confidently predicted it to be Sark. The lookout said it didn't appear to be Sark, and on closer inspection (luckily not dangerously so) this turned out to be true, and we were in fact approaching Guernsey. Embarrassed, I looked for the source of the error. It turned out, as usual in navigation errors, to be a case of garbage in, garbage out.

When setting up the machine in the morning, one of the first things I did was enter the date and time. I was so used to entering my date of birth that I had inadvertently sent us back to 1963, so all of our positions were based on one wildly inaccurate piece of data. It's a wonder that it worked at all – in fact, it would have been better if it hadn't, since then I would have probably found the error rather sooner. I suppose I could have used the Eric Morecambe defence: 'Listen, Sunshine – we are in exactly the right place, just not necessarily in the right decade.'

— AEROBATIC SIGNAL —

ALAN WILSON

Practising firing flares is rarely done and reading the instructions in an emergency may not be useful. I organised a 'flares day' a few years ago and had to step in very swiftly as two people were about to fire a handheld flare upside down: since you hold it tilted away from you, the bottom is tilted towards you...

On a similar training day many years ago we started when a biplane appeared and did aerobatics quite close, which was very impressive. We stopped and watched before it flew off and we carried on. Some weeks later I found out that the biplane had been booked to perform outside the window of an elderly lady in Clacton; the signal that he was in the right place was a flare...

— NOT A TANKER —

TOMMI JOKINIEMI

After an exhausting day of hand-steering in three-plus metre seas from Visby, Gotland, to Kalmar Sound, Sweden, we approached a combined marina and commercial harbour for a much-needed rest.

It was around midnight, when suddenly our AIS VHF unit gave an alarm of a vessel whose closest point of approach (CPA) was less than 0.2 nautical miles in ten minutes. Against the city lights in the rain I could see a couple of big ships with lit decks.

The tiny AIS screen on the VHF unit gave me the ship's name and I promptly called them on VHF: '*Fantasia, Fantasia, Fantasia*. This is S/Y *Anniina*. We are progressing under sail, approaching you from bearing 095° and have a CPA in ten minutes of less than 0.2 nautical miles, do you see us on your radar?'

'Negative.'

'We are a progressing under sail and seem to be passing close.'

'For your information we are a tanker...'

We concluded that they could not care less and carefully passed at a safe distance. I later double-checked their AIS status and realised they had said: 'We are at anchor.'

— OVERLY HELPFUL SAILOR —

SIMON VAGE

It was a beautiful day with a gentle breeze and I'd promised a good friend that I'd take her for a sail in my Moody 33 MkII. After a few hours of relaxing sailing, we headed towards the Helford River to pick up a buoy and put the kettle on for a cup of tea.

After a break, we hoisted the mainsail and set sail out of the mouth. Heading out, I decided to show off my local knowledge by pointing out August Rock and its dangers.

However, as we approached, an oncoming boat changed course to cut across our bow. I dutifully altered course, but as I did, the approaching boat again altered to cross my bow. This happened on three occasions, slowly pushing me on to the one rock I wanted to avoid.

Narrowly slipping between the August Rock buoy and the oncoming vessel, the other skipper called out: 'I've just come over to let you know there's a hellish rock just here, you need to give it plenty of clearance.'

Thankfully, I believe that my words of thanks to him were lost in the breeze!

— INTO THE BLUE —

KAY 'JAY J' BOMMER

Navigational apps are great as they make life so much easier and safer, but they are not without their pitfalls, as I discovered.

I sail an International Folkboat on the Schlei, a somewhat narrow and, in places, shallow fjord in northern Germany. Soon I came to appreciate the function of my app that allows me to set the colour of the water depending on its depth.

All I had to do was to take the 4ft draught of my beloved Santa Maria, add a small safety allowance and set my app to show all depth of less than 5ft in blue and the deeper water in white. As long as I kept well enough away from the blue parts on the chart, I would not run aground.

Having gained something of an expert navigator status after some seasons, my brother-in-law asked me to be his navigator on his boat during a trip on the Schlei.

Of course, I agreed. Simple enough to save him from grounding, I thought. To my utter surprise, the boat came to a sudden stop after only a few miles. Despite us being well outside the charted blue parts.

Only then did I realise that his Nicholson 35 had a draught of 5.5ft. I guess even the fanciest app doesn't dispense you from using your good old brain.

4
TO MOTOR OR NOT TO MOTOR: WE DIDN'T NEED THE ENGINE ANYWAY!

_____

— INTERNATIONAL INCIDENT —

EDWARD SUTTON

After many years, I am still embarrassed by a stupid oversight during the first trip in our newly home-assembled kit 19ft Seawych yacht. We launched it into Portsmouth harbour, hoisted sails and, with little wind, started the new 5hp outboard to push us out into the gently ebbing tide.

My wife and I knew the harbour from past adventures, but it was new to our two sons, who were excited to see warships on the quays. All was fine until the outboard spluttered, died and refused to restart, leaving us drifting along, making use of the light wind.

However, despite every tactic learned from dinghy racing, we drifted across the fairway towards the quays and in particular towards a US warship who had crew sitting on a board painting the hull. This activity seemed to have a magnetic effect on our boat which defied my efforts to restart the engine and frantically pump the tiller. The amused painting crew made ready to fend off our mast, but just before we created a potential 'International Incident', a furious harbour police launch arrived to tow us clear.

I then discovered the air vent on the outboard fuel tank was closed!

— SEAGULL SERENADE —

CHRIS WEST

For those of us who have been around boats for more years than we wish to remember, the Seagull outboard is ubiquitous. The basic design of this two-stroke was simple – a cord was wound around the centre of the exposed flywheel on the top in order to pull-start the engine. Having set the throttle, you would close the choke and 'tickle' the button on top of the carburettor to prime the fuel.

This procedure was pointless unless the easily overlooked fuel tap under the tank had been pulled 'on'. To start the unit, you had to pull the toggled cord mightily, which usually resulted in lashing the remaining passengers in the dinghy with the knotted end of the starter cord! Once the engine was running, care had to be taken not to allow any loose part of your clothing to be entwined in the exposed, swiftly rotating, flywheel.

Frequently in open anchorages I would wake to hear a dinghy drifting past. The conversation of those aboard the tender, were variations of the one below:

Tink-a-tink-a-tink-a-tink, wrirrrr

'Bloody thing won't start.'

'Have you got the choke closed?'

'Oh, of course I bloody have!'

Tink-a-tink-a-tink, wrirrrr 'Is the fuel on?'

'Of course it bloody is…!' wrirrrrr wrirrrr

'Have you primed it with the tickler?'

'YES!' wrirrrr wrirrrrpop

'Have you tried it without the choke?' wrir

'Look, if you're the bloody expert we'd better change places…' wrirrrr wrirrrr

And off they would drift into the night.

Ah the Seagull outboard. I often wondered in the morning if they ever got them started, though I confess I rarely bothered to check.

— A WELL-MOWN CARPET —

RICHARD CLUTTERBUCK

It was a wet walk that brought us into the chandlers, where I spotted the 2hp outboard. It had gone overboard and was now seized, so was very cheap. I decided this was a learning opportunity, and once home I took it apart to find out more. With the cylinder head off I could finally see the piston.

I felt free to try things I would not have considered on a 'posh' outboard, so I added oil to the piston and with a block of wood, a large hammer and a lot of force, the piston moved a little! Encouraged, I continued until the piston was completely freed.

I decided to reassemble the engine, to continue work another day, but wanted to show my wife progress, so took it to the hall by the kitchen, where my wife was. To show her how beautifully the piston now moved, I pulled the starting handle vigorously. The engine roared into life. The propeller spun fast, and dug a neat furrow in the carpet. I was delighted, my wife less so. The groove in the carpet remained for years and I still think my wife believes I did it deliberately.

— WHAT A COCK-UP! —

JOHN SOLOMAN

It was a glorious April day, ideal for the first sail of the season. It started swimmingly, but a few minutes after departure I noticed black smoke leaking from the engine bay under the cabin sole. Moments later, the hydraulic steering failed and then the engine stopped. We were now in serious trouble, adrift in a narrow fairway on a strong ebb tide.

About to make the DSC call, I hailed a passing powerboat, asked for a tow to the marina, and agreed terms. The crew and I fitted the emergency steering gear, set up the tow line and bridle and off we went – practically at planing speed – while we wrestled with the jury steering.

VHF communication was difficult. As we approached the dock entrance, we steered a little uptide to ferry glide in across the ebb, alarming our rescuers somewhat, but we shot the gate perfectly.

Thankfully, the smoke subsided and when the engine bay was cool, we had a look. The automatic extinguisher was never hot enough to discharge. The impeller was intact, the engine was okay and it started, but there was no cooling water. Then the penny dropped – I hadn't opened the raw water sea cock!

– JUST DON'T STOP –

CHRIS HANSON

After the 1991 Dartmouth regatta, to help on the delivery back I crewed the short-handed *Racy Lady* rather than come back on Tony Todd's *Eagle F1* with my crew mates. After motoring for 18 hours, we tried to sail, but the wind died and we put the engine back on... but no propulsion... no prop! It was fine until we had removed the load and it slid off the prop shaft to the bottom of the Channel.

I radioed *Eagle* who were a while behind; they said they would come and give a tow, so we sat drifting gently at Anvil Point. Along came *Eagle*, but only Andrew Kennedy was on deck. Where were the other five on board?

As the boat came close, at full blast from the deck speakers 'Thunderbirds International Rescue' blasted over the quiet sea and five guys, with paper hats, splashdown jackets back to front and brick fenders on their back, puppeteer'd up on deck... they still tease me about it, though considering the scrumpy I'm amazed they can remember it!

– TEMPERAMENTAL OUTBOARD –

GLENN JOHNSTONE

'We need to invite Brad again on our next trip,' my wife declared in exasperation. 'He always gets the dinghy motor started first time.'

'I can only do my best!' I retorted, still unsure of Brad's secret method. Is it his height? Something to do with the choke? There's always debate around the dinghy motor: Is it worth the effort of taking it down off the transom for only a short trip to shore? Does it have enough fuel for the journey? Shall we bother taking the kill-cord with us to dinner (always in my view) in a vain attempt to prevent theft, accidental or otherwise?

The night in question we were in Mljet, on the way back from a feast of Croatian lobster pasta and Pošip wine. Our yacht was anchored on the far side of the bay and I just couldn't get the dinghy engine to start. After 15 attempts I declared it must be flooded. We'd wait a few minutes and give it another go. Ten attempts later, my wife announced that she'd had enough and would single-handedly row us back to the yacht.

To her credit, we made steady progress across the bay. Any assistance I offered was rebuffed – I'd had my chance – and now my wife would save the day all by herself! After 15 minutes of rowing we were about to pull up to our yacht. I reached into my pocket to get the keys to the boat and... there was the kill-cord. Exactly where I put it before dinner.

— CHERBOURG REVERSE —

BRIAN CLEMENTS

Long ago, when a Westerly 33 was thought large, five friends and I chartered one from Lymington. Our navigator failed to show so it was down to me to find Cherbourg. Young, confident and inexperienced, I found the port after an uneventful night passage.

Then it unravelled. Entering the Grande Rade, a strong south-easterly headed us as we looked to cross to the marina. We motored, furling the sails, but the wind checked our course. Alarmed, we dropped our anchor, engaging forward gear to ease the strain on the ground tackle. The anchor dragged; the harbour wall neared. Our first flare failed. The second soared over Cherbourg, landing on the harbour lookout tower, startling its occupants. The French Navy came, towing us the short distance to the marina.

Next morning, a writ arrived, keeping us in harbour until payment of salvage. The charter firm advised flight. We sought the Lloyd's Insurance Agent instead. Release was secured with promise of payment of the salvage claim. A visit to the admiral saw removal of the writ with an apology that payment helped keep the French fleet at sea.

Back on board, my crew had solved the problem of the night before – the gear linkage had reversed.

— WHO NEEDS A PROPELLER? —

DON FITZROY-SMITH

I was crewing a Conway One Design back from Bangor to Conwy. The sail down the Menai Strait and across the Penmaen Swatch was uneventful until we reached the Conwy fairway, when the wind died. Though the skipper's Seagull started, we went nowhere.

After some hurried investigations, we soon found the problem. There was no propeller! We'd also forgotten the oars. We ghosted along until a passing yacht towed us to the nearest mooring that their draught allowed. Our mooring and tender were downstream, on the next trot; no club launch, no other help, and now the tide was ebbing strongly.

We were stumped – we had no means of propulsion or steerage; if we had no means of propulsion, how could we steer? None of us wanted to get wet by swimming for it, but luckily the skipper had an idea.

'While moored in a tideway we have steerage. If we veer our warps, we can do it.'

With all convinced, we turned to. Bending the long warps together, we passed the longest through the mooring-ring and back aboard. Then we slipped and veered until abeam of our mooring before putting the helm over. Finally, we secured to our mooring and recovered our warps. There was relief all round, but I never did discover why the propeller fell off...

— A WHEELIE BIN DISASTER —

DAVID HILTON

My Honda 2.3hp outboard motor had been difficult to start so I took it home for 'fettling'. Having fiddled around under the cowling and generally given things a bit of love I decided to see whether I'd achieved anything. In preparation I filled a wheelie bin with water and clamped the motor to one side of it, with the leg immersed.

The motor started first pull so, feeling pleased with myself I opened the throttle. The centrifugal clutch kicked in and the prop sprayed water everywhere, soaking me instantly so that I let go of the tiller handle. There was now insufficient water in the wheelie bin to steady things and the whole lot tipped over, drenching me to the skin with the outboard's propeller spinning madly in the air.

Only when I'd cleared up the mess did I remember that the motor is in fact air-cooled and doesn't need to be in water to run at all, so my wheelie bin full of water and subsequent soaking had been entirely unnecessary.

— SINGING PROP —

JULIAN BROWN

Some time ago I took possession of a new boat, a 26ft Cornish Crabber, about two years old. The boat was immaculate and I was very proud of my new acquisition. I had the vessel transported by road to West Wales where I live and had it located on the hard over the winter months, when I fitted some teak fixtures, electrical sockets, clock, barometer, an oil lamp and some other refinements.

Often, between jobs, I would give the three-bladed fixed prop a polish with some high-grade silicon polish that I had found in my shed – you could see your face in it! Over the years I've found there is little difference in many prop antifouls and the result on lift-out is exactly the same – covered in weed, slime and barnacles.

On launching in the spring, a high-pitched whine came from below at certain revs. Panic! I had the prop shaft alignment checked by two different engineers who told me exactly the same thing – I had a singing prop, which could be exaggerated by polishing and that it would go when growth started to build up on it, which indeed it did!

— OIL MISHAP —

COLIN FLOOD

With the boat out of the water and safely in its cradle for the winter, it was time to change the saildrive oil. I'd done it before, nothing would go wrong. I rammed a funnel into an empty oil container and knelt down to drain the old oil into it. Carefully loosening the drain screw, oil started to seep out and the screw slipped through my fingers and down the funnel where it lodged in the narrowest point and caused a total blockage. With a stream of oil pouring from the bottom of the saildrive and rapidly filling the funnel, I did the only thing I could do and put my finger over the hole.

I knelt there for a long time, thinking, like the Dutch boy with his finger in the dyke. I looked around, but there was nobody to help. Within sight, but well out of reach, was an old washing-up bowl with my tools in. I had no choice: I dived for it, leaving the oil to overflow the funnel and over the ground. I spent the afternoon clearing up.

5
HIGH AND DRY: WHEN THE BOAT JUST WON'T FLOAT

—HULL-DEEP IN MUD—

ROBIN HUNTER

The pilot books for Morlaix say the river dries and the lock gates only open at high water, and one hour either side of it, but it does not give the distance upriver to the lock gate. We found the entrance to the river, anticipating arrival at 1930 in time for the last lock opening. With an ebbing tide, however, we were making slow progress. The depth began dropping below 2m in places and I was becoming concerned. I had no option but to continue, as turning back would have meant drying out somewhere down the river.

Finally, at 2030, we saw the lock ahead of us. I radioed, but neither the lock keeper nor the marina office answered. A man on the shore shouted to us, saying that the river would dry out completely. We motored across to a waiting area and prepared to tie up alongside a wall. He continued shouting, so we motored back to the other side so we could hear him more clearly. He was the lock gate operator, and was walking home after his last gate opening.

Amazingly, he said he would open the lock gates to let us in. We motored back to the other side of the river. The tide was ebbing so fast that we hit the bottom and the boat stopped. While our navigational errors were clearly on display, we were not prepared to admit defeat, and with full power on, we inched forward, ploughing through the mud and finally broke through to the safety of the lock. One minute later and we would have almost certainly been sleeping at an awkward angle for the night. We felt that a bottle of scotch was the minimum payment!

—READY, STEADY, STOP!—

SUSIE MELLERS

My husband and I first took a boat out on our own from Mylor Harbour, chartering a 29ft Westerly Merlin. We decided on our first passage and that night's stop in advance, made all the tidal calculations and identified the buoyage. It took some time to squeeze all our gear and supplies aboard.

Having last been on a training boat with lots of eager crew and one person on each mooring line, our main concern was how we would manage with just the two of us, with no one to pass lines to. We planned in detail how I would slip the lines and my husband would motor out of the berth. We rigged and rerigged the lines and fenders (with much discussion as to length and configuration) so that I could release us and be back on board quickly.

Finally we were ready. The motor started happily, lines were slipped and I was feeling rather proud of our progress until my husband started shouting 'let go' with increasing frustration in his voice. I had, but we were not going anywhere. I shouted back, thinking perhaps the engine wasn't in gear. Finally it dawned on us that we had run aground in the berth. Our extravagant departure preparations resulted in our planned high tide departure slot having been and gone.

Sheepishly we concluded there was nothing for it but to put the kettle on and wait for the tide to turn.

—A SILVER LINING—

GORDON FYFE

A passage from Scotland to Spain some years ago required a visit to Dingle to revictual. Approaching Dingle's awkward entry late at night, I chose the Irish Cruising Club Directions from three possible sources. The instructions identified two pairs of buoys and directed a curved path between them round a shallow bank. Unsure of how big a curve, I ran aground just before low water.

I rowed out a kedge from the bow and about an hour later we floated off and arrived in Dingle marina just after midnight.

When I consulted the charts later, both showed a dredged channel directly between the pairs of entry buoys! When marina staff asked the next day when I'd arrived, I told him that it was that morning and paid for two nights rather than three. I still feel a little bit stupid, but at least I saved some cash.

– ROAD BLOCK –

JAMES DEASLEY

On a fine summer's morning, midweek, my new girlfriend Wendy and I played truant from work and drove to Maldon for a short sail. I had recently enjoyed a circuit of nearby Northey Island with my dad, so thought we could re-enact it. The water was quite high so I opted for an anti-clockwise route to cross the Northey Causeway before the tide dropped.

I didn't fit on the outboard, as I envisaged a quiet sail in the light breeze. As we neared the island we could see a long ripple in the water, marking the location of the causeway.

'We'll never get over that,' said Wendy.

I pooh-poohed that. However, the nearer we got, the faster the boat was carried towards it, and despite my efforts to sail away, the boat came to a juddering stop. As the tide dropped we were left parked, blocking the roadway.

A troop of small boy scouts walked over from the Island, to ask if they could help. Thanks, but sorry, no chance! A traffic jam built up. Embarrassed by the attention, we abandoned ship and sunbathed in a nearby field. A policeman on his bike arrived and wrote copiously in his notebook before departing without seeing us.

It was dark before we floated off, and a dense fog had descended. We motored to 'our' side of the river but had little chance of finding our mooring. We could hear one of the big gravel barges approaching, but could not see it, so we were relieved to spot another buoy, and spent a cold night aboard – no bedding, no breakfast.

We were very glad to regain our own mooring in the morning and drive home!

– AHH, IT'LL BE FINE! –

DON FITZROY SMITH

I was sailing with a couple of friends. We motored out of the marina and down the Caernarfon fairway before making sail in light winds. We enjoyed ourselves for a few hours before the wind gave out, so we anchored at Pilot's Cove for lunch. There were other yachts there at anchor enjoying the sunshine, and when the water in the channel allowed, they weighed in turn and made directly for the fairway buoy.

I looked up and commented, 'If they can go that way then so can I.'

'But have we got enough water?' my friend James asked.

'Yes, we'll be fine, we've done it before,' I confidently replied.

We weighed anchor and motored with me at the wheel, chasing the other yachts. Then it happened. There was a loud thump and we stopped, abruptly. The bow dipped, the stern rose out of the water and everyone was knocked off their feet.

James scrambled up and exclaimed in fluent Anglo-Irish, 'What was that?'

A quick look at the chart plotter gave him his answer. We'd somehow managed to hit the wreck of a barge, fortunately without sustaining any damage. Sailing is many things, but it's never dull.

— BREAKFAST WITH A BUMP —

GEORGE DUBOSE

Leaving Denmark for Sassnitz, Germany, with my crew, Rick, I noticed that there was an emergency harbour at Darßer Ort in the National Park Vorpommern. According to the cruising guide, the harbour had no facilities, plenty of mosquitoes and a silted entrance.

Skylark's AIS showed a German search and rescue vessel named *Theo Fischer* in the harbour. We radioed *Theo Fischer* asking if the entrance and harbour were deep enough for a 2m draught. They were.

We tied alongside the wooden jetty, had a nice dinner on board, watching the sun set while lighting a mosquito coil. After breakfast we motored out of the harbour, went about 200m and 'thump!' We hit the edge of the channel. Turning the boat back was unsuccessful and I was considering the dinghy and a lead line to find the channel, when *Theo*'s tender appeared.

'Only stopping for breakfast,' I shouted at the Germans.

Pulling us back into the channel, they told us the channel was dug a week before, and the buoys would come next week…

— FRUITS DE MER —

KEITH MAY

Several summers ago, my wife and I sailed in company with friends for our holidays, setting sail from Cherbourg on a bright July day. We were heading for Diélette, specifically for the moules-frites on the quay.

The Alderney Race was kind and we enjoyed a slowish sail catching mackerel and heading towards Diélette with our friends' boat five minutes ahead of us. We both knew we would be arriving just before low water, but the tides looked okay and as we are both bilge keelers and have relatively shallow draught, we confidently pressed on.

Through my binoculars, I could see our friends approaching the entrance and we carried on, organising fenders and ropes. When I looked a few minutes later, they were still in the entrance… They were aground.

Clearly the harbour entrance had silted, but I could see they were only just bobbing, and as we draw less than them by a couple of feet, I thought this was an opportunity to motor by with an appropriate but courteous military-grade raspberry.

My advice is to check exactly where the deeper water lies. For some reason, probably idiocy brought on by excitement, I chose badly. Drifting past our friends' port side with raspberries loaded and ready to deploy, to our horror, we very gently came to a stop. This created great amusement for our French cousins who, from the harbour walls, could now watch two British boats wallowing in the harbour entrance.

To the further amusement of the French, confirming that all the British are mad, I rushed down below, changed in to my swimming trunks and jumped off the back of the boat. The boat was only just aground and as each gentle wave lifted our vessel, I dug deep and pushed, and slowly moved her beyond the grip of the hump of sand. I climbed back on board when properly afloat and my wife motored us into the pontoon where we put the kettle on while waiting for our friends.

The moral of the story: Before deploying a military-grade raspberry at a friend who has run aground, always check which side the deeper water lies. Other French boats were sailing by on the starboard side, their crews grinning from ear to ear.

— WATCH YOUR UNITS —

ANDREAS FALLASCHINSKI

A few years ago four of my friends and I were sailing on the Ijsselmeer from Lemmer to Stavoren. A shortcut showed on the chart plotter, a channel between shoal patches of 0.6m depth. It looked small but adequate to cut a few miles off our trip, and the chart showed '3' in what we translated to be 3m – more than enough. Suddenly our boat came to a halt.

We managed to increase our heeling and with the motor in reverse we soon came free. No other boats were around that evening, and we would have been stuck for a long time or would have to call costly help. Later on we looked at the paper chart and quickly realised our error: The chart plotter on the charter yacht showed depth in feet, not in metres as we stupidly assumed.

All five aboard learned our lesson. We are now all extremely sensitive to depth below our keel and I hope that we will not run aground any time soon. Jokes abound about our embarrassing story.

6
FAMILY FIASCOS: DRAMAS WITH OUR NEAREST AND DEAREST

-TIN CANS NEEDED-

ED CROSSE

I have many happy childhood memories of family sailing holidays on the south coast but, as a parent, one stands out – for which I still apologise to my father, 42 years later.

We were in Salcombe, moored on the Kingsbridge Estuary. My father had a small 22ft Hurley yacht, just big enough for his family of five. I was the youngest, aged five, and as such had the privilege of sleeping in the main cabin – on the floor.

One night, during a gale, I decided to venture up on to the deck and climb into a large sail bag, tethered to the mast base. It was so warm and dry inside – despite the howling wind and rain – and I fell fast asleep. The following morning, my parents awoke to the horror of a child's empty sleeping bag...

I recall, so vividly, my father's crying voice: 'Ned! Ned! Where are you?! My God, he's gone!' And then, a few heart-stopping moments later, a wet-eyed, ashen-faced but indescribably relieved father opening the genoa bag to discover the smiling face of his little boy inside: 'Hello, Daddy!'

Now, as a father of three myself, when I go to sleep I place tin cans on every cabin step… Sorry, Dad!

— DOING A RUNNER —

DAVID PICK

I was reminded recently of a visit we paid to Lamlash some years ago. My wife and I plus our daughter and her husband had chartered a Legend 35 out of Largs and a visitors' mooring in Lamlash was our first night's stop. We piled into the inflatable tender and rowed ashore to the pub where we enjoyed a good meal and some games of pool. When we eventually returned back on board I thanked my son-in-law for treating us to the meal, to which he replied, 'I thought you paid!'

The outcome was that the following morning daughter and son-in-law rowed back to the pub where there was only a cleaner at home so a suitable deal was struck and money changed hands. I often wonder whether the publican got paid!

— SERVICE WITH A WOOF! —

BERYL CHALMERS

My friend, his wife and his dog, Popeye, were cruising around the east coast and had moored in Haven Marina in Ipswich. They'd arrived late in the evening so didn't have time to victual the boat for breakfast the next morning. My friend, whom I will call John to save his embarrassment, promised to be the good husband and to walk to the supermarket with Popeye in the morning for bread, milk and sausages, allowing his wife to have a well-deserved lie-in after two weeks of early-morning starts for the tide.

Bread, milk and sausages bought, he set off back to the boat – by this time it was nearly 1100. It was then that the plan started to unravel. Bumping into a couple of old work mates, John was persuaded to have a 'swift half' in the local Nelson pub, renowned for its real ale. Explaining that he could really only stay for a short while, his mates were having none of it and another round was ordered. When the third round was on its way, John realised he might be strung up in the rigging if he didn't get breakfast back to his wife, and so devised a cunning plan.

He put Popeye and the breakfast in a cab with a little note saying, 'Just having a swift one with a couple of mates. Popeye was happy to bring the sausages, milk and bread back to you!' When John eventually arrived back at the boat, Popeye was looking very pleased with himself, having been given his master's breakfast instead of Chum.

– PUSH ME PULL YOU –

PHILLIP CAVE

I used to sail my father's cruising catamaran, but there was one weekend I would rather forget. The boat was on the slip in a Woodbridge boatyard having had a leak repaired – or so I thought. When I first arrived, the tide was low and I got aboard with the intention of sailing off at high water. I put a kedge out to the low water mark to allow me to pull the boat out from the slip on the morning high tide, tying the warp to the timber pushpit.

I spent the night on board and as the tide came up in the morning, I noticed water was coming into the boat – the leak wasn't fixed!

When the boatyard arrived for work, they wanted to haul the boat up the slipway to take a look. The shipwright asked me if it was okay to start winching and I said yes.

There was a creaking sound, followed by a loud crack as the warp on the kedge tightened and clean pulled off the large timber pushpit. The shipwright and I just looked at each other, but I understood what his look meant – it meant, 'You gave me the okay.'

Later that day, I made a difficult phone call to my father. At least someone was happy – the boatyard got a bit more work out of it!

– BOTTOMS UP –

BRIAN NORTH

'When can we eat?' asked the kids.
'Nearly there,' I lied.

An hour later, we anchored in 2m. We draw a relaxed 60cm. Osborne Bay. Midweek. Alone, apart from occasional grim-faced yachties struggling eastward against the strongly ebbing tide.

'Can we eat now?'

'Soon,' I said. 'Why don't you have a swim?'

'Ooh yes, let's!' Excited screams of joy and splashing followed.

I declined the kids' invitation to join them. Having recently enjoyed three months' idyllic Med cruising, I was unconvinced of the merits of UK swimming. The kids emerged goosebumped and teeth chattering but ate lunch with gusto.

'Can we have another swim now?'

They slithered into their cold, wet swimsuits, and dived in again. But there were no screams of joy. This time it was screams of fear and pain that brought me quickly to the transom to behold our eldest standing up to her waist in water, blood pouring from her head.

What had happened? The ebbing tide had left us not actually aground, but nearly. I blame the tideless crystal-clear waters of the Med for seducing us. Had the bottom not been sand? It doesn't bear thinking about, does it? Well, actually, it does.

– MUM'S THE WORD –

TIMOTHY LONG

I'll be the first to admit that it wasn't a kind thing to do. Mum isn't a huge fan of sailing, at least not when it's windy, but we had booked a holiday in the Mediterranean as a family and Dad and I were looking forward to doing some exciting sailing together. Mum was happy as could be in the tranquillity of a quaint little harbour, but Dad and I wanted her to experience the same rush of adrenaline as we did out on the waves.

Heading out to sea, however, with the wind building, the flogging sails unsettled her equilibrium. Dad and I couldn't wait to get going though and set full sails anyway. With a satisfying amount of power, the boat heeled over and was flying along.

It was then that the forecast gusts started to arrive. I was having a whale of a time, but Mum was less convinced, so we set about putting a reef in. The wind and waves continued to build so we put in another reef.

Eventually, the boat speed was back down to two knots and a smile had returned to my mum's face. She still tells the story of the storm she survived, but perhaps a happy Mum might ensure that we come back next year…

— A LESSON IN SIPHONING —

THOMAS ROBINSON

It was my first big adventure with Dad, a night sail from Pwllheli to Dublin. We motored in flat calm and eventually had to refuel the outboard from a jerry can.

Dad proudly announced that he had a new, foolproof method for siphoning; using a second tube to blow into the airspace at the top of the can and start the siphon flowing – no sucking needed. He set it up and I blew hard; only to be rewarded with a spray of petrol back into my face!

Dad panicked, threw me onto the cockpit floor and proceeded to dowse me with water for ten, miserable minutes. As I lay shivering in the dark, he told me not to feel too guilty, better luck next time and at least we hadn't wasted too much petrol!

After 10 years of believing that I was somehow to blame, he recently confessed. It was actually his fault as he had pushed the second pipe too far into the can. He then had the cheek to tell me that I should be grateful, that he had taught me a valuable lesson: 'Always double check everything'... especially if your dad is supposedly in charge!

— STRANGERS IN THE NIGHT —

RAY LUPTON

I was the charter skipper for an Italian family of four; two adults and two teenagers – a girl, and a boy called Roberto. There was a second boat containing the rest of the extended family. The second boat was owned and skippered by Mattaus. We anchored outside the entrance to Gaios on Paxos. It was crowded, but we managed to find some space, some distance apart from each other. The teenage boys wanted a late night out in Gaios so Mattaus agreed to pick them up in the dingy when they were ready to return. The call came at 0500. Mattaus collected them and dropped Roberto off on my boat. Roberto went to his cabin, and at the same time that he realised he was on the wrong boat, two large gentlemen appeared.

Roberto leapt into the cockpit screaming for his uncle to rescue him. He tried in his limited English to explain it was a mistake. After much apologising from Mattaus, the situation ended happily.

— DON'T FORGET YOUR CREW —

MATTHEW DIGGLE

We had almost finished putting away our gear on the yacht we'd chartered when the harbourmaster wandered up and offered to help guide us out of its rather

tight berth. We quickly stowed the last few items and got the engine going. The harbourmaster walked the bow along the pontoon and then gave us a shove off. I was acutely aware that I was being observed as I carefully reversed away, then spun round quite neatly and headed out of the marina. The lines and fenders were being brought in when I remembered that one of my sailing instructors had told me that the last step in all manoeuvres and evolutions was 'put the kettle on and make a cup of tea'.

It was at this point that we realised we had more cups than crew members. Meanwhile, back in the marina, and much to the harbourmaster's amusement, my wife returned from the car with the last few bits and bobs to find the berth empty and the boat nowhere to be seen. As I rather sheepishly turned the boat round and headed back to collect her I remembered another piece of advice I'd been given, and which I think will now always stick in my mind: 'Before casting off, do a headcount.'

— A LITTLE VOICE —

SYLVIE DUBOIS-MARSHALL

Sailing with a small child has its challenges, but our daughter, then aged four, was normally adept at settling into her bunk with her Lego (potential for bilge-related mishaps but none so far), books or a story tape.

We were sailing gently towards Loch Fyne, the sun shining. Tea and warm scones with strawberry jam in the cockpit for the parents, daughter busy in the cabin. Suddenly, we heard a little voice, 'Belfast Coastguard, Belfast Coastguard, Belfast Coastguard, this is yacht *Murmur*, yacht *Murmur*, yacht *Murmur*.'

We smiled at each other, slightly surprised, and thought 'what a clever little girl we have' (during the last week at sea, she had been listening with interest to the regular exchanges on Channel 16).

There was a short silence, and then, 'Yacht *Murmur*, this is Belfast Coastguard, are you in need of assistance?'

A longer silence. We looked at each other. Her father, always calm and collected, looked very uncomfortable. After what seemed like a long time, he took the handset and replied, 'Belfast Coastguard, this is yacht *Murmur*. Please disregard our last transmission.'

There followed a lengthy discussion about appropriate use of the VHF!

— A HUMBLE APOLOGY —

COLIN LANGFORD

My wife and I were at a boat show looking at our dream coastal cruiser. We removed our shoes before stepping on board as is custom and left a few bags of stuff we'd bought at the show with them. Hours later, having left the boat and taken all our bags, we stopped to consolidate our purchases. My wife looked in one bag and then looked at me accusingly.

'I didn't see you get a new pair of shoes…'

'I didn't!' I protested.

'Then why are your old ones in here?'

Only they weren't mine. We'd picked up one too many bags on leaving the boat, in one of which another of the viewers had stored their shoes for safekeeping. If the person who had to walk around the show in stockinged feet is reading this, I apologise.

7
A CLOSE SHAVE: HOW DID THEY GET AWAY WITH IT?

———

— GOING UP IN THE WORLD —

JAMES FROST

My friend Walter's hearing is not great and mine is probably worse. When we're sailing two-handed, we rely a lot on hand signals. Offshore on a dark night on my Westerly GK34, I fumbled with a shackle and lost a halyard up the mast.

In an effort to make the loss good, I hurried aloft as fast as I could, me climbing and Walter winching like mad. I was close to the top when I realised the pressure was on my armpits and not the crotch area. The bowline was level with my glasses.

It was then that I discovered I had hooked on to my lifejacket and not the climbing harness, which I'd strapped on in a big hurry. The next few minutes should have been comical. I was pointing at the deck and shouting, 'Down! Down!'

Walter was giving me a big thumbs up and shouting, 'Keep going! You're nearly there!'

It was a long way up the second time, very carefully connected to the climbing harness.

— A SHARED TEASPOON —

SIMON TEMPLE

Many years ago, a group of us from work chartered a Jeanneau Sunfast 36 from the now long-closed Sunsail base at Largs, for a weekend trip.

It was the start of the season and when we arrived there was almost no cutlery on board. The thought of eating breakfast with a shared teaspoon didn't appeal, so we spoke to the base manager, who suggested we took what we needed from the identical yacht on the next berth.

Next day we had a great sail through the Kyles of Bute to East Loch Tarbert. Shortly after we arrived, another Sunfast 36 came in, with a crew doing a weekend training course. We overheard them complaining bitterly about the lack of cutlery. We sneaked off shamefacedly to the pub without owning up!

— MAST MISHAP —

HARRY BLATHWAYT

It was the Three Rivers Race, 1967. We'd made the Stracey Arms mark before the tide changed, had shot Acle Bridge both ways and Potter Heigham Bridges on our way up, lowering the mast without dropping the sails.

We were now on our way back from the Hickling Pleasure Boat buoy. My brainwave of rigging a trapeze to Striders, our 18ft Broads half decker, may not have produced more speed but had certainly added to the gaiety of the race. We'd enjoyed a soldier's wind across Hickling Broad and there was even a chop as night fell.

Now we were approaching the two Potter Heigham Bridges again with the strengthening wind up our chuff. We slipped into our practised 'shooting the bridge' places: Paul, my older brother, on the tiller in charge of the crutches, Clive and Mickey on the paddles and helping as the mast descended, with me disconnecting the gooseneck and controlling the jib halyard.

The bridge was approaching ever faster, and with the halyard untied the 20ft mast should have been dropping smoothly. Only it wasn't; it had stuck. The pivot pin in the tabernacle had cut a keyhole shape owing to the added weight of the trapeze, which meant the mast was resting on its foot. Realisation dawned on me.

Paul at this time was facing astern to guide the mast into the crutches he was holding. I shouted a warning. The confused faces of Clive and Mickey could be seen in a glimmer of moonlight as the mast met the span, clearing the jam immediately so the mast fell without the calming effect of the halyard, which I'd let go of.

Dropped in sympathy with the mast was the tan cotton sail that covered those young upturned faces. In the quiet that follows all such incidents the transistor radio played Procol Harum's 'Whiter Shade of Pale': 'We skipped the light fandango, turned cartwheels 'cross the floor, I was feeling kinda seasick…'

The mast was in one piece, but a lump of rotten foredeck had been lifted by the mast foot. The crutches had not fallen in the river though, which was some consolation. We recovered and paddled under the low arch of the old road bridge as if all was as we expected.

Although it took more effort than normal, the mast was raised and we sailed on to finish the race in the dawn's early light.

— A WHEEL OF A TIME —

SIMON JAMES

My wife and I took possession of our dream 36ft yacht as the winter weather set in. The first opportunity to take the boat out was from the marina berth to the hoist. I enlisted a couple of friends, the engine checks were done, the lads organised the fenders, and the mooring lines were readied.

We were off with a touch of reverse and slowly backing out. The lads busied themselves fending off and I went to turn the wheel, only to find to my horror that it was not there. Where there should be a wheel was simply a stump of binnacle. The wheel, I remembered, had been put in the cabin for safe keeping.

The lads were now relaying positional instructions and getting a little anxious as the boat was getting close to the adjacent pontoons. I hurled myself into the cabin, grabbed the wheel and was back behind the binnacle in a trice, where I thrust the wheel on to the axle.

To my surprise, with the now reassembled wheel, we did not hit anything. Even more to my amazement, when we were discussing our performance afterwards, the lads were unaware of my little drama. They thought the skipper's slightly erratic performance was down to nerves. I could have kept my secret and nobody would have been any wiser.

— MOB FINALE —

ROB WHELAN

We chartered a motor cruiser on the Hawkesbury river in NSW, Australia, 25 years ago. With two families and four kids on board, we were approaching

Brooklyn pier. At low tide the wharf was high above us. As we made contact, the foredeck crew leaned on the pier to fend us off. Engaging astern to stop us, the prop walk (my excuse anyway) took the stern away from the pier, and my mate moved from vertical to flat and fell into the water between the boat and a barnacle-encrusted pier.

We retrieved him unharmed (he did not even lose his glasses) as the entire restaurant above the pier applauded – our audience had watched the whole thing.

— LOCKER LEGS —

PAUL CLARKE

One of the ironies of 'Windy' Wellington, New Zealand, is that whenever we have a longer race the wind drops. So, one fine Sunday, with six aboard our Farr 9.2, *2 Low 4 Zero*, the spinnaker started to droop and it was time to get out the light air sheets. These are kept in a cavernous cockpit locker full of fenders, brushes and other paraphernalia. Not being used for a while, they had inevitably migrated to the furthest, deepest corner.

So I handed over the helm and leaned waist-deep in to locate them. Unfortunately, the relatively narrow opening activated the trigger on my lifejacket. It self-inflated, simultaneously sealing me firmly in the entrance, pinning my arm away from the deflation valve, and forming an acoustic seal. The rest of the crew, busy chatting as there wasn't much sailing action at this point, were unaware of my calls for help.

Eventually, vigorous waving of my legs signalled my fate and I was unceremoniously pulled back out. The race was abandoned for want of wind some time after.

— DRESS FOR THE OCCASION —

MICHAEL DAVY

We three, on a bareboat charter in Croatia, had a medical emergency. In the gloom of the cabin Karen had mistaken superglue for eye ointment. We diverted to Tisno, a tiny but crowded harbour in the southern Kornati, and found a space inside the harbour wall.

Brian jumped ashore with the bow line, while Karen – with a firmly glued eyelid – followed him, leaving me in the cockpit. The stern swung away from the wall with the wind. Undaunted, and as Karen clearly couldn't assist, I swung over the rail, preparing to jump on to the quay with a stern line.

At this point, standing on the toerail, I realised I was barefoot, the rail was sharp and hot, so I leapt. Backwards. Still holding the stern line, I fell between the hull and the quay wall, scraping my back on the barnacles on the way down, and then up again, as I bounced off the bottom. With the stern now swinging back against the wall, I needed a quick exit. Helped by Karen, and bleeding from my scraped back and punctured soles, I scrambled on to the quay.

I couldn't help noticing Brian, still holding the bow line, grinning like a Cheshire cat.

— A SINKING FEELING —

LIZ SAUNDERS

Our first sail of any distance was to the south coast of Ireland, having travelled from Cardiff Bay, motor-sailing to Dunmore East. We were feeling very proud. The boat performed really well, the engine had been overhauled and was sounding good. All was well with the world. Suddenly, something began to vibrate horribly in the engine. Had we caught a lobster pot line?

We shut the engine down just in case and anchored. Middle age had begun to catch up with my husband and donning a wetsuit after putting on weight took skill, brute force and clouds of talcum powder. Hubby jumped into the water but floated, and couldn't get far enough under the boat. A weight belt to his midriff would help. 'Throw me a rope, I can lower myself down,' he said confidently. Weights attached and rope in hand, he dropped down into the water again.

With a splash, he plunged beneath the surface, clutching the rope. Amid vigorous but ineffective splashing, he began to look oddly panic stricken. He was rapidly running out of rope and, wearing ten kilos of lead, was sinking fast. I confess that only then did I realise I'd not fastened my end of the rope to anything.

I just managed to grab the end of the rope before it slithered overboard, and made it fast. A relieved, exhausted man in wetsuit and weights clambered aboard, while I tried to stop laughing. As it turned out, there was nothing wrong with the prop. An engine mounting had worked loose and my husband had needlessly walked the plank. Lesson learned.

– HOLDING ON –

EILEF J GARD

It was early spring, and the sea was at its coldest on this south-west corner of Norway. Our yacht was in its berth just below our house. I popped down to fetch something, wearing thin overalls over light clothes.

The marina was still under construction, so I had to find a secure foothold on a log as I put my hand on the rail, ready to step aboard. I took three seconds too long, giving the boat time to be pushed away. I braced myself for a very cold dip, and feared that my mobile phone in my pocket would drown. But, just as I was stretched out horizontally over the water, the mooring line came taut and the boat stopped drifting. There I was, feet on shore and hands on the boat, with no chance to escape the situation except to take the plunge.

But wait! My phone! With just one hand on the rail, I managed to fish out my only – albeit humiliating – hope for a rescue and called the first family member I found, my daughter.

'Mum!' she cried, 'Dad is falling into the sea!'

They panicked and came running, only to stop dead and bend over in laughter when they saw the hapless sailor.

'Oh come on, I can't hold on any longer,' I shouted.

When it was over, my wife regretted not having run back to fetch the camera, though I was much relieved.

– ALMOST A MUDDY END –

RICHARD HOPE-HAWKINS

Having just repainted the decks of our 35ft ferro-cement ketch *Brimstone*, one of Mike Peyton's old boats, I didn't want to drag the anchor chain across it and make a mess of all my hard work. How else could I get the anchor chain from the pontoon on to the boat on my own, with no one around to help?

Then inspiration struck… I picked up one end of the chain and began to loop it around my neck like a giant necklace, as climbers do with their ropes. It was getting heavy, but I reckoned I could cope with the full weight of the chain for a few minutes.

It was only as I was midway through stepping from the pontoon on to the boat that I realised just how stupid I was being.

As the boat moved under my increased weight, I tottered between success and oblivion. Gravity and chance were on my side that day and I landed with relief on board, but visions of me slipping and being buried head first in the mud at the bottom of Liverpool Marina have haunted me ever since.

— A SKIPPER'S PREROGATIVE —

TERRY KEMMANN-LANE

I've sailed with Keith on his boat at the end of the season for years. This year, we laid up the boat in Leros Marina, using the lazy line and warps from the quarters to the pontoon.

This left the stern about 7ft from the pontoon. We were all packed up and I had carried the bags across the passerelle just at the time that the taxi was due to take us to the airport. The passerelle would not stay across all winter; fortunately, there was one boat between us and the quayside, so Keith said he would cross the 2ft gap between boats and alight on the quay that way.

I went aboard the adjacent boat and helped pull the two together. Keith leant across and grabbed the side lines and settled his feet on his own toerail, whereupon the two boats began to part. Within a second, Keith was horizontal, toes on toerail, hands on side lines. It was clear he wouldn't be able to maintain this bridge long enough for me to take a photo and his cries of 'Do something!' left me wondering what.

Then it came to me: if I got back on to the quayside, I could push the neighbouring boat out and thus close the gap. First efforts simply made the two boats move away from the shore as Keith acted as a solid horizontal link. But I pushed harder with the risk that I'd also become horizontal between the quay and boat. Gradually they began to close up, and Keith hinged into a 'touch my toes' stance and then made it from boat to shore.

— USE YOUR HEAD —

MARTIN DOXEY

Harry was snoring loudly in the fore peak, leaving me solo at the helm. We were motoring south about four miles north of Holy Island when nature called. I scanned the horizon and went down to the heads. As I turned in the heads my jeans belt loop caught the door handle and pulled it off. This was bad enough but my attempt to push the handle back on succeeded only in pushing the door catch spindle out the other side of the door.

Grim reality hit me – I was locked in and we were approaching the shore at six knots! I started shouting and banging but to no avail – Harry is a deep sleeper and was not hearing me over the engine noise. Screaming and banging as hard as I could had no effect either.

Then I remembered the mobile phone in my pocket. I called him and got a rather bleary 'hello'. He quickly came to, checked we were clear and then let me out. Phew!

— WHALE SPOTTING —

ALISTAIR YEAMAN

A few years back, for my 50th Birthday, my wife and I decided to combine my lifelong ambition to see humpback whales in the wild with my love of sailing. We booked a yacht charter in the Pacific islands of Vava'u north of Tonga. In preparation, we studied the islands and planned an itinerary of all the places we wanted to see.

One of the stopovers was Hunga Tonga island, which is the rim of a sunken volcano that has formed a beautiful tropical lagoon. The pilotage into the lagoon was restricted to one narrow channel, with a pyramid-shaped rock just below the surface on the port side and a dog-legged shelf, just over a boat's

width, on the starboard side. Given the obvious dangers, we intensively studied the passage ahead of the holiday.

Eventually, the time came and we approached the entrance to the said channel. To say we were nervous was an understatement. My wife took her position at the bow, to look down into the crystal clear waters and give me directions at the helm.

We approached slowly and, at the moment we entered the channel, a humpback and her calf came to the surface not 20ft aft of the boat.

I turned and watched her, then after a few moments I turned back to concentrate on the task in hand, to see my wife over the bow shouting, 'Well done, that was tight but you got through it'.

Only upon reading this will she know that there was never any element of skill involved, only luck. But I did get to see a wild humpback whale at close quarters!

8
DINGHY DISASTERS: BIG COCK-UPS IN SMALL BOATS

———

-NOTHING TO SEE HERE-

BILL BRIMBLE

It was time for the mid-season scrub, and the Westerly GK34 was positioned on the Saltash Sailing Club scrubbing berth on the River Tamar. The owner, with me among his crew, did the hard work and then we waited for the tide tide to return.

'Don't worry, skipper, we will keep an eye on the boat as the tide returns,' we assured the owner, who had to attend to some urgent business.

It was a lovely evening and we were watching the Thursday evening club racing and did not spot that the inflatable dinghy, left alongside the boat, had become trapped under the bow with the rising tide. No amount of hauling on the painter would move the trapped dinghy. We eventually recruited some weighty bystanders to stand on the stern, and attached the club rescue boat to the painter. With full power and a tremendous whoosh and cheers from the gathering crowd, the dinghy eventually popped out, thankfully unharmed.

By the time the skipper returned, the crowd had dispersed and everything was back as it should be.

'Everything okay?' he asked.

'Oh yes, skipper. Just fine,' I lied.

At least I've confessed now.

— LEARNING THE HARD WAY —

SIMON LUND

We'd never sailed a catamaran before – only monohulls and boats without dinghy davits – but we set off for a bareboat charter to Bora Bora anyway. Having arrived at the island of Raiatea and received a briefing on the boat, we were told that when making a passage from one island to another, we must remove the outboard from the tender.

We then had a one-hour lesson with a French instructor to get used to handling the cat. 'No, no, no,' she reassured us. 'Do not worry. Leave the outboard on, it will be fine.'

The next morning, off we went for a passage with the dinghy in tow, crossing between Raiatea and Huahine in a 20-knot easterly trade wind that was kicking up 2m seas. Two hours in and BANG! I looked back to see the tender flipped over by a wave and the red fuel tank disappearing over the horizon.

We sheepishly called the charter base. The 'engine on' thing is only okay if the boat is in the davits. We learned the expensive way.

— FLYAWAY DINGHY —

SUSIE POTTER

In our first year of yacht ownership, we were sailing our Beneteau First 405 home after a night on a mooring. The wind was gusting 25 knots down the western Solent. The dinghy was still in the water and so, rather than religiously stow it away on board, we thought we'd live a little and tow it home like other people did. We unfurled our genoa for the downwind trip and away we went.

All was well until we realised the short Solent chop was dumping water into the tender, which was becoming very heavy. Apparently nobody had taken the bung out for it to self drain. The point was reached where we had to act. We tried to heave the dinghy up the yacht transom to tip it, but we didn't have the strength.

Not to worry, a cunning plan was hatched: We'd attach the dinghy painter to the main halyard and winch it up, draining the water and enabling a safe recovery. The dinghy started to creep up the transom, dumping its water. We were triumphant. This was until an especially strong gust launched the now much lighter dinghy into the air. Still tethered to the main halyard it soared, dived and flew! It took 15 minutes to capture the thing.

Passing boats yelled at us and pointed, compounding the horror. We never forgot the bung again.

—KNOT WITHSTANDING—

MIKE HOWARD

I can pinpoint exactly where our bad luck started. We had changed the name of our new boat without the correct ceremony, resulting in an engine rebuild, rerigging and a list of sundry other jobs.

Having purchased a dinghy and outboard big enough to carry five people and a dog, the budget was spent. With the dinghy towed astern, we approached our mooring in Mengham Rithe in Chichester Harbour on a falling tide. Suddenly, I saw the dinghy sailing away over the barely covered mud flats. My knot had come undone!

I knew that if we didn't retrieve the dinghy quickly we would lose it, and there was no way we could afford another one. I gave chase and told my wife that she needed to hook the boat painter at the first attempt, or we'd either be marooned or lose the dinghy – probably both. Skilfully, she recovered the dinghy and we managed to get back to the mooring safely.

As I looked back over the now-uncovered mud flats where we had been only moments before, I could see the erratic track marks of our bilge keels in the mud. It had been a close shave! My birthday present from my wife that year was Colin Jarman's book *Knots & Splices*.

– ROMANCE IN THE RAIN –

PETER SOLLY

I admit it. I was trying to impress her. She was my girlfriend visiting for the weekend, and clearly the best thing to do was to take her out on the very old 24ft plywood catamaran I'd just bought. It was December, raining, and for some reason I'd left the dinghy outboard on the boat. But no matter; I'd row us in my other recent purchase – a rectangular glass-fibre dinghy, which was probably older than I was. What could possibly go wrong?

The tide runs fast on the River Exe and the catamaran was about 100 yards offshore, on a mooring in the middle of the stream. By the time we arrived, the wind and tide were pushing strongly downriver. A simple ferry-glide out would do it, I figured.

We set off, and as soon as we got into the stream it became clear this was going to be a difficult row. Despite my efforts, the cat got further and further away from us. For three quarters of an hour, I rowed my rectangular bathtub as if my life depended on it.

Eventually, we managed to make the shore a mile downstream from where we started. It didn't matter that it was a long, muddy walk back to the car: by this stage, just reaching dry land felt like a major success.

She never did get out to the boat, and a few weeks later the cheap rented mooring chain parted and the catamaran was washed up on a rocky shore and then written off by the insurance company. But all was not lost: she is now my wife.

— THE SUBMERSIBLE DINGHY —

NICK JOHNSTONE

Years ago I chartered a pretty 29-footer for a week's cruise. Having spent the first night rolling sickeningly at anchor, I was keen to get off as soon as possible. 'What should we do with the dinghy?' my girlfriend asked.

'We'll tow it. It will be fine,' I replied.

We were soon on a broad reach, with a good breeze. However, the boat seemed oddly heavy and slow.

'Where is the dingy?' my girlfriend suddenly shouted.

I looked back astern, and there was only empty sea. I cursed myself for not getting it on board and secured properly. I was gloomily pondering the ten miles back to the marina, followed by the embarrassing conversation with the charter company, when I spotted the dinghy painter, still tied to the cleat but straight as an iron rod.

After a brief pause my dinghy gracefully surfaced behind the boat, like a submarine! It had inverted, and the suction created by pulling it along had caused it to submerge completely. Hoping no one had noticed, we secured the dinghy and set off again, this time cantering along at a fine pace.

— TENDER LOVING CARE —

LESLEY BLACK

It's was the late 1970s, quite early in our sailing careers, and we were off to the Hebrides in *Tillew*, our trusty Sabre 27. The crossing from Northern Ireland had been challenging, as below decks I'd acted as putative navigator, one-woman bucket chain for two seasick offspring, comforter-in-chief to Fletch, our Dalmatian dog, and provider of regular nourishment to the skipper up in the cockpit, dividing his time between battling the elements and cursing the autohelm.

In dire need of rest, we made for Ardminish Bay on the Isle of Gigha. Today it's a popular spot, but back then it was just a few moorings, a handful of buildings and a short wooden landing platform for the ferry to the mainland. Happily I dropped the anchor and turned to survey my crew – the kids, now well rested, starving hungry and bursting to get to the beach; Fletch, not so well rested, but also bursting, for different reasons; and the weary skipper, yawning loudly but already pumping up the dinghy.

Overcome by maternal instinct and an urge to bank brownie points against possible future trials, I told him to get some rest while I took them all ashore. He didn't argue, though he did launch into a lecture on tying up the dinghy with a bowline on a long painter, so as not to inconvenience others.

'We'll be fine,' I said, and off we splashed.

The bow had barely touched the pier when the crew were all up and away. Knots never were my forte and my bowline kept slipping so I made do with my usual round turn and as many half hitches as I could manage. It wasn't pretty, but it wasn't going to slip. Unfortunately, it also used up a lot of painter. But what the hell, there was nobody here to inconvenience and the tide was well on the rise, so no problems there either.

It therefore came as a shock when, after a couple of happy hours exploring, eating ice cream and feeding the parrot at the hotel we returned to the pier to find the dinghy missing. Unbelieving, I stared around the bay. Nothing. I walked towards the pier and then I noticed something very odd indeed.

Halfway along it, my mountainous knot was definitely still in place. And as I went forward, all became clear, for there, trapped below the walkway, its grey rubber flanks bulging up at me accusingly through the wooden slats and making strange squeaky noises, was my dinghy. Obviously, the rising tide had carried it under the planks where, due to my abandonment of the long line policy, it had stuck fast rather than drifting on through to the other side where I could have retrieved it. I had indeed inconvenienced a yachtsperson – myself.

Luckily, after another hour or so of beach activities, we found the pressure had eased and out it came, sporting a few scratches and wood splinters but otherwise unharmed. The skipper, roused from sleep by our noisy return, looked at his watch in amazement.

'That was great,' he said, 'but you've been gone for ages! I don't know what you found to do for all that time.'

Well, he knows now...

— STILL WATERS —

ANDREW ROBINSON

It was a sunny, frosty January day on Lake Windermere. I had driven up from Manchester to check on my Leisure 20, which was moored behind Belle Isle. I couldn't afford a smart inflatable tender then so I used our Mirror dinghy instead. The lake looked so beautiful, tranquil and still; not a ripple on the glassy surface.

I eagerly launched the dinghy and started rowing out. I waved happily to the wardens who had started gathering for some reason on the shore, and they smiled back.

I put my back into the rowing, building up quite a speed. I was flying along until, with a crunch, the boat came to a juddering halt. Pulling myself together, I stood up and looked to see what I had hit – was it a stray mooring buoy or a boat? Nothing.

I then looked at the unusually calm water – the lake was frozen solid!

As I sheepishly rowed back, the penny finally dropped as to why every warden had looked so cheerful.

— WITHOUT A PADDLE —

TIM BULTITUDE

This takes place 11 years ago, when I owned a lovely little Wing 25, *Waterwing*. My son, aged 13, and I had spent the night anchored off Stone Point in the Walton Backwaters. In the morning we set off just after low water with a stiff south-westerly blowing. When leaving the Backwaters there are two red cans which, around low water in a south-westerly wind, it is best to give a wide berth to, as they tend to blow over the shallow water. I didn't, and suddenly we were hard aground.

No problem; the tide was rising and soon there would be enough water to float us off. Deciding it would be a good idea to drop the anchor upwind to stop us blowing further on to the shallows, I set off in the dinghy. I reached a suitable spot and dropped the anchor over the side, along with both oars!

I was soon blowing very fast downwind and, despite my best hand-paddling efforts, I passed *Waterwing* with a very concerned son staring at me. Luckily I had taught him the basics of VHF distress calls. He had the very good sense to press the magic red button. This summoned the Backwaters warden and the Harwich inshore lifeboat who picked me up and returned me, very red-faced, to *Waterwing*, while my son was having a nice chat with Thames Coastguard.

So my advice to fellow sailors is (a) stay away from the red cans, (b) tie your oars to the dinghy and, most importantly, (c) make sure your crew can use the VHF.

— TOO SLIPPERY BY HALF —

JACK HANDLEY

I work for my local harbour and was on the quayside when I noticed that someone's tender had come adrift from their boat. I chuckled to myself that whatever hitch they had used couldn't have been very good.

I hopped into the harbour work RIB to go and retrieve it, and soon had it towing alongside my boat as I took it back to the yacht. Once alongside, I jumped up and tied the tender's bow line back on to the vessel, feeling like a smug hero.

Job complete, I sauntered aft back to my RIB, only to see both the tender and my RIB drifting down river. It seemed the slippery hitch I had used was rather too slippery. Luckily, my work mate wasn't too far away and he brought them both back to me, but he hasn't let me forget it yet.

— LOBSTER POT TANGO —

OLIVER L SHAW

For reasons of practicality my dinghy, which doubles as my survival craft, is an inflatable, and I leave it fully inflated and tow it astern when on passage. Being a belt-and-braces man, I also rig a 'lazy painter' as a safety line.

On this occasion I was sailing along the Anglesey coast, single-handing my 20ft trailer-sailer; a glorious beam reach on port tack under full plain sail in bright sunshine, cracking along and touching six knots on both the log and the chart plotter, which is not bad for a 20-footer – especially when towing.

I was periodically bailing because on that tack at that speed water slops up the outboard well and into the cockpit. I failed to spot a lobster pot buoy under the sail in time, and the lazy painter fouled it, with the result that we were abruptly anchored by the stern. We promptly swung downwind, so we were now anchored by the stern and on a dead run, in a gaff cutter under full plain sail, in a decent blow. It took me a little time to get myself out of that mess!

— CAPTAIN UNDERPANTS —

MARK CHERRILL

I was on holiday with friends from work and we had chartered a yacht in Croatia. After a gorgeous day's sailing, we anchored in a beautiful bay alongside a cool beach bar. It was early evening so we were all getting ready to go ashore for drinks and dinner. I was already in my finest attire for the evening when the skipper asked if I had tied the dinghy to the boat earlier. I happily confirmed that I had.

'Better go and get it then,' he replied.

I looked up to see it floating away further into the bay and towards the wide sea beyond. I stripped down to my pants, dove in, and retrieved it to cheers from the crowd at the bar, so when we all finally made it ashore there was a most welcome line of drinks waiting for us. We all had a splendid evening with sore heads the next day.

9

MOORING MAYHEM: GETTING TIED UP IN KNOTS

———

— OFF THE WALL —

LEONIE STEER

With a gale forecast, we sailed up to Newport on the Isle of Wight for a few days to escape the bad weather. All went well. We tied up opposite The Bargeman's Rest, took lines ashore and a mast strop to tilt *Shen Shui* towards the quay. We sat and slept through five tides.

I was woken suddenly on the third day by a metallic twang and an alarming lurch. The boat lurched again as I put my bare feet to the floor. In the pitch-dark I yelled at Tony that the boat had fallen away from the quay, supported only by her mooring warps.

We dashed out into the drizzle to find an alarming list and a large gap between *Shen Shui*'s deck and the wall. Grabbing extra warps we scrambled ashore and attempted to tighten ropes and add extras, to no avail.

Tony suggested getting the main halyard and tying it to the bollard, but the halyards were stuck under the mast strop and the angle to the top of the mast would have pulled a rope up and off the bollard. The tide was falling fast now and the boat was in serious danger of falling.

I went to shelter in the women's showers, but a few minutes later Tony yelled that he had found a strong post outside the Harbour Office. Could I go back on board as I was 'the lightest one' and get the topping lift and a shore line out of the lazarette? With a 4ft gap to the wall and the boat wobbling precariously on its keel, I managed it, without even losing the shackle pin.

Tony tied the shore line to the post, joined it to the topping lift and, with the boat 'secured', went back on board. He started winching and slowly the boat began to lift towards the vertical. But dawn was coming and with it, traffic. We nearly decapitated a cyclist on his way to work as our line now was about 60ft long and straddling the municipal car park. Cars were also a hazard, as they narrowly missed driving into and breaking our lift rope.

The solution? I hung the bucket and our fenders on the lines, much to the bewilderment of commuters. Eventually, the tide rose and we removed the evidence of our mishap, and at high water we left, probably never to return!

— IGNORE AT YOUR PERIL —

THERESE LABOS

I decided it would be a good idea to spend two weeks afloat alone on my husband's sloop. He prepared a list of dos and don'ts that I chose to ignore, which, I must now admit, had embarrassing consequences.

The boat was moored bow-to at Marina Bay in Gibraltar. I flew out from London and made myself at home. I had difficulty clambering aboard so I eased the stern rope.

Two nights later I was woken from sleep by loud banging on the hull and loud yelling, 'Therese, your boat is sinking!'

The bow had got caught beneath the overhang of the pier as the tide rose and the stern was dramatically up in the air. All the crews of neighbouring boats came to my rescue by boarding and crowding the bow and attempting to push the boat off to free it, which they eventually achieved, and all this within close view of a vociferous audience of late-night revellers who cheered on the proceedings as loudly as possible.

Maybe I should have read the list after all.

— HIGH AND DRY —

HUW GIBBY

My mate Pete asked if I'd help him free a mooring rope around his prop, and I agreed! The mooring was a mile up-river in a muddy creek, which dries out, so we went in another friend's dinghy an hour before high water.

We couldn't free rope by turning the engine over, nor with a boat hook – the muddy water with zero visibility didn't help. I suggested I use my weight on the bow to raise the prop out of the water. Pete agreed and asked me to keep an eye on the quickly dropping tide whilst he hung over the stern. It took an age to free the prop, and sitting on the pulpit watching Pete in his attempts to free it, I totally forgot about the dropping tide!

Celebrations were short-lived as we were high and dry. Pete yelled, 'Quick, jump in the dinghy, before it's too late!' But it already was!

We tried to row through the mud with the water three or four dinghy lengths away – but failed.

Panicking that we couldn't return to the boat, we hauled on a mooring chain to pull us back – phew! We spent an uncomfortable night on a 20ft yacht with no bunk cushions and no food.

— DON'T PULL THAT PLUG! —

WILLIAM H HOLLIDAY

Sailing with young grandchildren persuaded me to have my 1988 Westerly 'MOT-ed' by experts. The rigging and roller reefing were replaced, the anti-slip decks repainted, the engine serviced and the pungent holding tank – which my wife detested – was duly replaced.

'We fit these to the Oysters,' I was told. 'There's less pipework, operation is faultless and they're odour-free'.

Afterwards, I booked a maintenance bay for a pressure wash ready for the season. It was high water on a beautiful afternoon. Everything was going according to plan when it came to tackling the final patch towards the stern. There appeared to be some paper stuck on the hull. Anxious to get finished, I gave it a sharp tug as it resisted the pressure washer.

A plug of paper came away and all too late I realised the source was the 'empty' holding tank. An absolute torrent ensued. I couldn't believe a holding tank could contain so much. It was accompanied by a vile stench, which pervaded the atmosphere, including the raised area overlooking the maintenance bays where my wife was standing.

Those seated within range moved instantly, one enquiring, 'Is that your boat?', to which my astonished wife replied: 'I don't think so.'

I have never used a pressure washer so frantically.

— NEWTON'S THIRD LAW OF MOTION —

CHRISTOPHER HILL

On our first family flotilla we had a gentle first day sail from Skiathos to raft up stern-to a rocky breakwater. The instructions were simple – drop the main anchor and reverse to within about 5m of the rocks, then take out the kedge in the dinghy and drop it in the rocks before tightening everything up.

We were the last boat in with a decent audience and sent Edward, our ten-year-old, to anchor with the kedge. As he stood up and started to swing it to throw it on to the rocks I shouted 'Noooo…' but too late. The kedge went a little way forwards, the dinghy went at speed backwards and Edward went down somewhere in the middle.

He could swim and no harm was done as he surfaced like a spouting whale. Having learnt this early lesson in physics, Edward is now a senior software engineer for a multinational company.

— PROP WALK LESSONS —

ROB WARD

I used to potter about in a semi-project boat; the combination of an underpowered engine and my timidity meant 'prop walk' wasn't something I worried about very much. When we finally upgraded to a 'proper' boat, we headed for the Graving Dock in Cardiff Bay for our first night on board.

Anxiously I nosed into the dock with the engine just ticking over; there was a slight breeze over the stern but nothing too dramatic. I decided to turn the boat round before mooring up. More or less at a stop, I turned the wheel to starboard, and almost made it, but just needed a light touch in reverse to continue the turn... Oh no! Prop walk sent the stern emphatically back to starboard, undoing the turn but a boat length closer to the end of the dock.

Despite increasingly frantic manoeuvres with wheel and control, the inevitable happened – bang! My beautiful boat hit the dock wall. £250 to fix (the boat that is; the dock was unharmed).

– SOMETHING TO PONDER –

MIKE THORNTON

My first long mission was blighted by a lack of wind. I was running short of fuel so I gave the Coastguard a quick call for advice and it was problem solved: 'Go to Hastings,' they said, 'and tie up like the fishing boats.'

I couldn't find anything in the pilot guide about Hastings but no worries; in I went and tied up just like the two fishing boats, with just a bow line. It took me forever to find fuel, but I wasn't concerned. When I returned to the harbour a large crowd had appeared and my mast had disappeared from view. Oh dear!

The fishing boats had gone and the only thing left in the harbour was my boat on a 45° slope held only by the bow line. A guy standing near me summed up the situation succinctly: 'Who moors a boat like that?'

An excellent question and something I decided to ponder in the pub!

– SINK OR SWIM –

RON STODDART

Many years ago, in our small riverside town in the south-west, a very old sign on the quayside gave an obsolete harbourmaster's telephone number to ring before placing a new mooring. Turning to locals for advice, I was told to wait until evening and place a marker in an unused location. If after a few weeks there were no objections I could then lay a suitable mooring.

We set off towards the location of our intended mooring with a very heavy lump of concrete with marker buoy attached in our small tender. Once on the spot, and well clear of any other moorings, it was with some effort that I heaved the concrete overboard, and almost threw myself overboard with it in the process.

Imagine our confusion and horror, therefore, as both the buoy and concrete lump proceeded to float downstream towards all the moored yachts. Chasing after it, we eventually retrieved it, thankfully without damage, but also without our mission complete. The concrete lump, it transpired, contained enough air to make it buoyant, aided by the buoy.

We headed back to shore in search of a heavier weight, and were met with gales of laughter; the locals gathered in the garden of the riverside pub had enjoyed front row seats for the entertainment we provided.

— TIED UP IN KNOTS —

KEVIN WEST

During a recent sailing trip to Croatia we were joined by some friends. One evening we needed to secure a long line ashore and as I prepared the tender my friend Pete offered to tie the two coils of rope together. I told him the outcome of other friends' attempts at this task, which had resulted in lines parting at the first sign of tension. Pete found this very amusing but assured me he knew what he was doing. He tied the two ends together in what was a very secure-looking knot, and off to shore we went.

I secured one end of the line to a large rock and let out the rope as Pete rowed us slowly back to the yacht. Suddenly I ran out of line and was holding one end in my hand.

'Pete,' I asked, 'what happened to your fantastic knot?'

'It's still fastened tight,' he said, 'I can see it here right by my feet'.

Bemused he soon realised that he had tied two ends of the same coil together!

— ICE-CREAM DISTRACTION —

KELLY RASHLEIGH

We had just taken possession of our 1994 50ft Endurance, *The Esperance*. We decided to go straight out for a sail as the boat was due to be hauled out the next day for a refit. We had our young children with us but also a couple of friends, which gave us enough hands to test out a few things.

After a bit of pottering we decided to head to Cowes for a celebratory ice-cream. It was busy on the water so we called ahead; Shepards Wharf said they had spaces but by the time we arrived the marina was full. The activity on the radio was relentless and we could hear that we weren't the only ones looking for a mooring. Fortunately Yacht Haven had a space on the harbour wall.

It was high water springs so we were glad to see the wall empty as it made manoeuvring an unfamiliar boat easy. We tied up and the kids led us straight to the promised ice-cream shop. We had a lovely time taking a stroll along the beach, stopping to skim stones and collect shells.

A couple of hours passed and we thought it best to head back. We soon realised our mistake: the boat was now a long way from the top of the wall. When we tied up we were so distracted that we had forgotten it was a wall and not a floating pontoon. Fortunately for us our friends had returned in time to slacken the lines as *The Esperance* dropped.

We will always be grateful to Matt and Kate – if it wasn't for them that would have been the most expensive ice-cream ever.

– DRAGGING TO WINDWARD –

KEITH GREENFIELD

On a recent charter cruise to the Hebrides we had taken shelter in Canna harbour in near gale conditions. We had dropped anchor as all visitor moorings were taken, but our 25kg Rocna was holding nicely. Three of us then left the boat in the dinghy to stretch our legs ashore, leaving the others on board to keep anchor watch.

On reaching shore we looked back and observed in horror our yacht apparently 'drifting' forwards, into the wind and towards its anchor, threatening to pick up the hook! For a moment we just couldn't compute what was happening and began yelling back at the remaining crew members still on board, hunkered down below.

Fortunately one of the crew just happened to be looking in our direction and saw us waving our arms and they all came on deck and then realised the yacht was on the move under engine. The engine had been switched on to heat water with a few revs forward and someone forgot to press the button on the throttle to keep her in neutral! How would we have explained dragging our anchor on to the windward shore in the insurance claim?

— A SIDEWAYS TWO-STEP —

DON FITZROY SMITH

We were in Douglas marina, berthed on an angled finger pontoon with limited space astern to manoeuvre. Narrowing our escape route was a large, rusty barge with a heavy workboat alongside. Prop walk takes my 1988 Victoria 34 *Triptych* off to port; we hoped the small river flowing into the marina would take her to starboard, but the cross wind was proving to be a problem, so I reviewed Duncan Wells' *Stress-Free Sailing* for inspiration.

Our efforts started well enough. The berthing master managed our lines, we fended the workboat off our stern. Then the wind grasped *Triptych*'s bow and off we went downwind. We moved down the fairway, broadside on, rather red-faced. At the mercy of wind and water, we nudged the workboat astern and our pulpit kissed the pushpits ahead as we went downwind and downstream, until clear of the berths.

Thankfully, there was no damage to anyone and we seemed to evade a local judging panel with their scorecards. Or did we?

10
THE COVER OF DARKNESS: EMBARRASSING EPISODES THE NIGHT CAN'T HIDE

———

— BLINDED BY THE LIGHT —

PETER ROLT

Some years ago a friend and I were sailing back up to Bristol from Falmouth. I usually liked to do the trip in one go, so we may not have been at our most alert by the time we were somewhere between Ilfracombe and Foreland Point at night and spotted bright red lights directly on our intended course.

Nothing appeared to be on the chart and whatever it was, it was big and brightly lit so we would have to go around it. We tried to give it a wide berth, but we had no idea how far away it was or which direction, if any, it was moving in. The lights did not get any dimmer and remained too close to our course for comfort. How big was this thing?

I don't remember how long we spent trying to avoid it, but I do remember the mixture of relief and red-faced embarrassment when I realised we had been trying to sail around Cardiff airport, the bright lights of which, perched as they are close to the shore, had utterly confused us.

— HOW'D THAT HAPPEN? —

GRAHAM HUGHES

I recently completed the ARC with three friends of 30 years' standing. During the trip, we replaced the sheets with longer ones in order to set up the twin headsails. One morning, I came up on deck and noticed one of the stanchions was bent backwards at an extreme angle. For the next week or so, we all proposed a number of different theories as to how this might have happened, but we never got to the bottom of it.

After 22 days, we arrived in St Lucia safe and sound with no further mishaps and retired to a local café for a celebratory breakfast. The subject of the bent stanchion came up again, but this time a crew member said he knew exactly how it had happened.

One night when he was on watch, he'd decided to put a reef in as the wind was picking up. Having let the sails out to ease the strain on the furling line, he then started to winch in the sail. Unfortunately, he'd picked up the original short sheet, which had been loosely attached to the rail. As he winched, he met some resistance but thought it was just the pressure of the wind. It was then he realised his mistake. Luckily, the skipper found the whole thing as funny as the rest of us!

— BRIGHTLINGSEA LIGHTS —

SARAH O'REILLY

One September weekend in the late 1980s, I sailed with my parents in our Macwester 26, from Maylandsea to Brightlingsea on the River Blackwater. It was our first family weekend cruise in Dad's new pride and joy. He had carefully chosen a short hop for his inexperienced and semi-reluctant crew.

By the time we approached Brightlingsea, darkness had set in. Dad was at the nav station, hunched over his paper chart; I was helming, aiming for the leading lights; and Mum was looking out for the elusive flashing buoy that marked the moorings. The leading lights were getting alarmingly close but we obeyed Dad's instructions to keep going, when the bilge keel nudged into soft sand and we came to a gentle halt.

Dad tried to reverse off, but we were held firm and spent the night neatly parked. The next morning, we were shocked at how close the moorings were and, once we refloated, made our way over. My teenage self was mortified when the harbour staff asked if we had had a pleasant overnight trip from France. I hid down below as Dad explained that we had only come from Maylandsea.

— WHAT IS THAT? —

LIZA DODDS

My husband and I were motoring our 38ft Hunter *Legend* from La Spezia to Elba overnight. Several nautical miles ahead of us we saw a huge lit-up structure. From behind it came another vessel, a bright white light above it. What was it doing? The lights were getting brighter and Mike insisted it was coming toward us, and fast.

I rushed to the radio, only to discover that I'd turned it off earlier in the watch, as the white noise of another vessel had become annoying. I turned it on and straight away a stern and increasingly urgent voice was telling us to keep two miles away from the structure, which was, it turns out, an oil platform and safety patrol boat.

I apologised profusely and promised a westward course, while Mike opened up the throttle and motored rapidly away. On reflection we realised we had both made school-boy errors. He should have checked Navionics more carefully, as the structure was marked with an exclusion zone, and I shouldn't have turned the radio off.

— MOONSHINE —

CHRISTOPHER SMITH

It's not often we choose to make a night passage, but we had a problem. The 'up-to-date' charts of the Black Sea have their own black holes and after touching ground three times trying to find a way into an estuary in the Ukraine I decided our best option was an overnight passage northwards to Odessa.

It was a starlit night, there was a gentle wind, no waves and warm temperatures: what could possibly go wrong? Being a late-to-bed person, I took the first watch, while Cocky, my Dutch sailing mate, got some rest.

Not long after midnight I retreated to the quarter berth with my Kindle. I was shortly interrupted by a call from the cockpit.

'Help… there's a large sailing boat coming straight for us and it's moving fast.'

I came and watched a pale yellow sail with a steady bearing on us from the east. It got larger and larger and I decided it must be a fast-moving catamaran on collision course with us. Then it became semi-circular.

'Cocky, isn't the rising moon so beautiful?'

— ON THE GAS —

GEORGE DUBOSE

While sailing from Helgoland towards 'the Gat', at 0300 I spotted what looked like a 900ft ship moving east ahead of us. It appeared to be a superstructure with a white bow light.

I kept a close eye on this vessel, which seemed to be moving very slowly. As my chart plotter was not showing the ship's position or AIS information, I couldn't get a clear read of its intended course. Apparently we were several miles north of the vessel.

After an hour, when we were much closer, I considered whether to try and cross in front of the vessel or behind it. I began to think it was anchored, possibly waiting for a tide change. When I could no longer see the white light on the bow, I picked up the binoculars. Finally, I could see that the superstructure was not a ship, but a gas platform. Moving not at all.

— RUDE AWAKENING —

PHILIP CAVE

We had moored our First 29, a fin-keeler, in the Bosham Channel for years, so decided to have a night on the quay to avoid dinghying out. Mooring up on the late afternoon high tide, we laid some heavy objects such as anchors and water containers along the deck against the quayside. We tied the main halyard to a fixing on the quay, to ensure that the boat leant against the quayside when the tide went out. Then it was off to the pub. Returning at about 2300 to settle for the night, we felt happy but forgot to check how the boat was sitting.

At about 0200 we were woken by a sudden jolt! I panicked and rushed up on deck stark naked and found, to my horror, the boat leaning away from the quay. I had a vision of it lying flat as the tide went out.

Thinking quickly, I put a mooring line around a post on the quay and around our winch and with every inch of my strength, slowly winched the boat back to the quayside, completely forgetting I was naked. No one was around at 0200... or at least, I hope so!

— FOG OFF ROSCOFF —

PETER KERSEY

It was time to return home from our cruise. We were up at 0400, ready to cross the Channel from Roscoff in daylight. The clear sky was full of stars. At 0445 we were ready to cast off, when dense fog descended, reducing visibility to a couple of hundred yards. I declared this to be radiation fog, which would clear at sea. So we set off, rounding the Port of Bloscon breakwater with its light glowing eerily.

Due to limited night vision, the skipper decided to helm, while the mate directed using his phone's Navionics app, away from the chart plotter and AIS at the nav station. The fog and swinging compass made it difficult to keep a steady course. Heading towards the starboard side of the deep water passage, we heard a large engine, travelling fast and close. A high red light appeared and what looked like two steaming lights! The skipper turned to starboard at full throttle. The vessel thundered past and we breathed a sigh of relief. But not for long.

A large fishing boat then passed with just its port and steaming lights visible. These must have been deck lights, though, one above the other! We had an AIS transceiver so the other vessels may have spotted us. As for the 'radiation' fog? Well, that continued for another 20 miles.

— THE BIG SLEEP —

RICHARD PEARCE

It was around 0200 when I pulled up in my taxi at the address in west Hove. My passenger, a middle-aged gent, was already saying his goodbyes at the door to a group of people after what seemed to have been a very convivial party. He got in and gave his destination as a little village close to the coast, a few miles east of Brighton Marina. I hadn't travelled far when I saw in my mirror he was fast asleep on the back seat.

As I passed the Palace Pier, the sudden 'bleep bleep bleep' of my lifeboat pager alerted me to a lifeboat call-out, and the need to get to the marina sharpish.

I was first to arrive at our boathouse and on answering the phone, found our tasking was to a yacht that had run aground under the cliffs just east of the marina.

Other crew arrived and soon we were speeding off on our Atlantic 21 lifeboat. It was a calm, foggy night and the yacht's skipper had tried to use his new GPS to find the marina entrance, but it had been set up with the wrong datum and led him too far east.

We managed to tow him off the rocks, but he'd also somehow got a rope jammed round his rudder and prop, so the tow back to the marina was a slow process, as the yacht kept trying to turn to port. On arriving back at the boathouse after a couple of hours, one of the shore crew asked, 'Who's the guy asleep in your car?'

In the midst of the red mist that affects all lifeboat crew when the pager bleeps, I had totally forgotten my passenger. I carefully got back into my taxi without waking him, turned off the meter, which was now over £50, and gently drove to the address he had given me.

Arriving outside his house, I turned round and gave him a nudge. 'We're here, mate,' I said jovially and gave him an estimate of what the fare should have been. Still in a dozy state, he paid without question, but I could see that the early-morning sky, where dawn was beginning to show, was causing him a little confusion.

As I drove away, I pretended I hadn't heard him ask, 'What time is it, mate?'

THE SAILOR'S SIN BIN

11
TOILET HUMOUR: WE SHOULDN'T LAUGH, BUT...

———

— NAPPY HOOLIGAN —

TERRENCE KEARNEY

When leaving Cherbourg with my wife and very young son, our stores included a pack of disposable nappies. As these items became full, disposal overboard was decided upon. As a Merchant Navy officer I was fully aware of MARPOL (marine pollution), so cleared the cotton and its smelly contents away from the plastic.

As we approached the UK, this practice stopped and the remainder went into a bag for disposal in Cowes. After tying up at the Folly trots at 0100 and loading the tender, the carrier bag — now quite full — was placed in the tender for the run to Folly pier. While passing a pristine Sunseeker gin palace, the outboard coughed and spluttered. Thinking I may have picked up seaweed around the prop, I thought a small tilt of the outboard would clear it and I could throw the weed to one side.

This time, however, it was not weed but the contents of the bag that my son had tossed overboard! The gin palace now looked like a brown spotted hyena.

THE SAILOR'S SIN BIN

We recovered what we could from the sea and made a hasty departure. My only hope was to pray for a downpour. I never did go back to check.

— A DROP IN THE BUCKET —

KURT JEWSON

On a beautiful Cornish summer's day, my ten-year-old son and I decided to take our boat out for a sailing and fishing trip around Mount's Bay. Not long out of Porthleven, my son uttered the now-legendary words, 'Dad, I need a wee!'

Ordinarily this wouldn't pose too much of a problem. Our boat is an open dayboat, so 'over the side' is the norm. However, the boat was heeled over and, given that his mother would kill me if he fell in, I advised him thus: 'Kneel down, wee in the bucket, then throw it overboard.'

Now, I must say that I had a bit of love for this bucket, having spliced a length of Hempex on to its handle, whipped the other end and generally make it an object of much fuss. So you can imagine my dismay when as my son was 'finishing up', I saw the bucket fly through the air, splash on the surface of the sea, capsize, take on water and slowly disappear into the depths, never to be seen again. 'But Dad, you said, wee in the bucket, then throw it overboard!'

— THE CRITICAL MOMENT —

CHRIS MARDON

My wife Veronica and I were motoring across the Channel from L'Aber Wrac'h to Plymouth last August after several weeks' cruising our Dufour 40 *Spook* around south Brittany. Our third crew member, George the autopilot, was volunteered to take on the tedious task at the helm. He is a Raymarine 6000G and is an amazingly reliable and skilful helmsman. We had risen at the crack of dawn to ensure a daylight passage home so at 1100, I was ready for bed. Veronica would sleep after I arose and before we hit the busy shipping lanes. Imagine my confusion when my peaceful slumber was suddenly turned into a nightmare.

Veronica was shouting at me and I was pinned against the side of the hull, the regular 'slosh slosh' of the water passing the bows now a hubbub of slapping waves. I looked aft from the forecabin to see Veronica in the cockpit with her trousers round her ankles, struggling with the helm. I could see the horizon rushing past out of the companionway hatch and *Spook* was listing hard to port. I struggled into the cockpit to find *Spook* doing tight circles at seven knots.

The pandemonium was caused by George switching from auto to standby at the most critical moment for Veronica when she was on the loo. With no hand to steady the helm, the prop wash had turned the rudder to full lock with the engine at full cruising speed. The remedy was very simple: throttle back the engine, get on course, hit George's auto button, throttle back up to cruising speed and pull Veronica's trousers up!

– BONNET DE DOUCHE –

RICHARD AVENT

We were in Brest on board our new catamaran with our newborn son. Consequently, the days started early and I walked up the deserted pontoon to an equally deserted shower block. Brilliant, no token required. I went into the first cubicle, stripped off, hung up my clothes, put my wash bag on the tiny shelf seat by the door and pressed the button with my palm while trying to avoid the immediate high-powered jet of freezing water. As I was probably the first one in, I anticipated it would take a minute for the hot water to find its way through the system. A few minutes later, it was still stone cold. Hmmmm...

THE SAILOR'S SIN BIN

I unlatched my door and poked my head out, still no one around, so I hopped out naked and worked my way round the empty adjacent cubicles pressing the buttons in turn. As I stepped out of the final cubicle and made for mine, its door slowly swung closed and its latch fell down. I frantically rattled the handle – it was locked fast.

I weighed up my options: Climb over the door? Impossible, the gap wasn't big enough. Do my best to cover my modesty and try to explain to the girl in reception in 'Franglais' what had happened? Streak back down the pontoon back to the boat?

It was then that I remembered my wash bag; maybe there was something in it I could use to pry open the latch? I laid on my back and wriggled as far under the door as I could while praying no one walked in at that moment. I managed to get my finger tips on the shelf and successfully pushed the bag on the floor and then pulled it outside. A frantic search ensued and hey presto, a pair of nail clippers with a nail file attached. I jammed it into the latch and gently turned it – success!

The hot water had arrived and after a lengthy shower I strolled back to the boat with a grin on my face – who would ever know? Assuming no one did walk in while my head was under the door, that is…

— SOAKED THROUGH —

JOHN TYLOR

My friend Don and I anchored near Brisbane where my wife joined us for the next leg of our sail north. Despite having been on yachts before, marine toilets remained a mystery to her. Nature called and she disappeared below. After a long silence, a voice called up, 'Which tap do I turn on?'

I gave concise instructions and waited. The next question came, 'What do I do now?'

Don now replied, 'Have you opened both ball valves?'

'Yes!'

'Well, pump harder!'

Now vigorous pumping, and a loud pop followed immediately by, 'Oh no!'

A minute later, a very damp wife appeared and swiftly jumped overboard to rinse off. I went to survey the damage. The outlet ball valve was closed and the hose, pressurised by energetic pumping, had separated from the anti-siphon fitting. The contents of the bowl were spread across the roof.

By the time I'd cleaned up, Don had finished the beer and my wife was freshly attired. At least the heads had never been so clean.

— THE PORCELAIN SHRINE —

PAUL HOUGH

It was 20-odd years ago and I'd just bought my first little sailing boat with my good friend John. The broker showed us around and explained the heads, emphasising valve lever positions, which didn't make sense to me, but hey ho!

Next morning, after several celebratory ales the previous night, we were motoring down the Suffolk coast and I sensed a rather pressing need to try out the heads, so we agreed on the lever positions.

'Well, that's what he said,' John confirmed a little hesitantly.

Afterwards I vigorously attempted to pump my offerings away from the porcelain shrine.

'It's not shifting!' I yelled to John, who was peering in to investigate.

That was the moment the resisting rubber valve chose to spring back with a vengeance. I was covered: hair, face, clothes... A victim of my own doings.

Stifling a guffaw, John talked me out of jumping into the water. That, dear reader, was my introduction to messing about in boats.

— A MESSY BUSINESS —

OLIVER L SHAW

The idea of using a square of astroturf for training a dog to do its business on the bow of a boat is a good one, but it didn't occur to me in 1985 when I was trying to yacht-train my puppy.

On one occasion, we were rafted up alongside two other yachts at Porlock Weir. With indisputable canine logic, the puppy decided that since Master preferred that it did its business on the foredeck, well away from the cockpit, no doubt he would like it even better if it used the foredeck of the boat next door. Fortunately, there was no one on board at the time, and I was able to clear up before the owner returned.

— MORSE CODE RESCUE —

GEOFF EVANS

During a delivery trip from La Palma to Antigua we decided to do single watches at night. My three-hour watch finished at midnight and I handed over to Natalie, who was on 1200-0300. I retired to bed for my nine-hour snooze. Natalie's watch passed without incident and at 0300 she was relieved by John.

At 0500 John woke me up and asked me to come on deck. What could it be? The boat sounded the same, the wind was around 20 knots, and the sea state was the same as was the wave direction.

'I am sure I can see a light glowing rhythmically SOS,' said John, 'but I can't see where it is or how this could be.'

I let my eyes adjust to the dark and looked. He was correct; there was indeed a rhythmic SOS coming from somewhere, though not out at sea. Perturbed,

I walked around the deck and found the source to be coming from the starboard crew head. I went below to investigate. On the floor outside the head I noticed the door handle. I knocked on the door and heard Natalie plead, 'Get me out of here!'

I replaced the handle and opened the door to find a rather disgruntled but relieved crew. Natalie had come off watch, filled in the logbook and gone to the loo. When she went to open the door, the handle came off in her hand and the male part fell onto the floor outside the door. She called out and banged for a while but – as those of you who have crossed the pond know – the background creaking and squeaking is quite loud. Once tucked up in your cabin wearing earplugs, it is difficult to hear other sounds.

Natalie had resigned herself to a long and uncomfortable off watch when she had a Eureka moment. She grabbed the emergency torch and started flashing SOS out of the window. We now have a spare rod in each head, allowing escape should the same happen again. We now also check the grub screws on each handle as part of our daily boat checks.

– NEIGHBOURLY SWAP –

PETER GUINAN

We were enjoying flotilla sailing in the Ionian. That night we tied up using lazy lines and so were stern-to the quay, with another boat alongside us. We had a chat with them and retired to bed.

In the morning there was a wild cry from one of my crew who was up on deck. Our neighbour's dinghy was full of stinking sewage. I had forgotten to pump out the holding tank the day before, and whenever any of our crew had used the heads during the night, the overflow matter had shot out into our neighbour's tender.

We could hear them moving about and expected them up on deck at any time. Fortunately they were with the same charter company as us and had an identical dinghy and outboard. We quickly swapped tenders, and hid the smelly mess behind our boat until we could quietly clean it up.

They came on deck, we had a pleasant chat, they had breakfast and left. I often wonder what the outcome would have been if they had come out of their boat a few minutes earlier.

—BLACK TEA, PLEASE—

PETER REID

Many years ago my friends and I were on our way to the Public Schools Sailing Championships on the Gareloch. We were to charter Billy Doherty's *Ain Mara* from Belfast. We loved the anchorage in the Narrows near Tighnabruaich, and this year we didn't go aground.

We ran out of milk on day two, however, so I rowed ashore and got some from a farm – warm from the cow, in used lemonade bottles with no tops. There was no fridge but we cleverly tied string around the bottlenecks and hung them over the side in the sea to keep the milk cool. Later when we came back from the pub we stood in a row to starboard and emptied our bladders, not thinking till we saw the three little bits of string over the toerail below us.

Somehow nobody wanted cornflakes the next morning, and we drank our tea black. We anchored off McGruers of Clynder, and that evening we had visitors aboard and served them cocoa. This is my apology.

—MORSE CODE RELEASE—

OSCAR O'SULLIVAN

During 2021 sailing season preparations, I had to use the loo. Given the COVID-19 pandemic, the club and toilets were closed. Without informing my skipper, I headed for the public amenities in a portable container block. The cubicle had a deadbolt lock and when I tried to leave, I could not unlock it.

There was no answer from the skipper so, with much deliberation, I called 999 and requested the fire service. Despite some confusion an engine was despatched. My freedom came when, thinking my rescuers were outside, I tapped SOS in Morse code.

It must have been where the deadbolt was positioned. Someone heard and pulled down on the handle, releasing me to explain myself.

ALSO AVAILABLE:

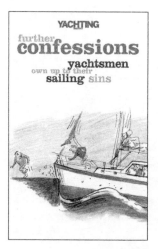